Action Wealth System

How to Be the Best You Can Be, Create Multiple Streams of Income, & Make your Money Work for You

GEOFFREY SEMAGANDA

Founder, *Action Wealth Academy*

◆ Action Wealth System ◆

Copyright © 2014 by Geoffrey Semaganda

All rights reserved. No part of this book may be reproduced or transmitted in any form or by any means, electronic or mechanical, including photocopying, recording, or by an information storage and retrieval system without permission in writing from the copyright owner.

This book is published by:

ActionWealthPublishing.com

Printed and bound in the United Kingdom.

Although the author and publisher have made every effort to ensure the accuracy and completeness of information contained in this book, we assume no responsibility for errors, inaccuracies, omissions, or any inconsistency herein. Any slights on people, places, or organisations are unintentional.

ISBN-13: 978-1497302402

ISBN-10: 1497302404

ATTENTION CORPORATIONS, UNIVERSITIES, COLLEGES, PROFESSIONAL ORGANISATIONS:
DISCOUNTS ON BULK PURCHASES AVAILABLE. FOR MORE INFORMATION, OR TO FIND OUT ABOUT SPEAKING/TRAINING AVAILABLE, PLEASE CONTACT THE PUBLISHER.

Editing, interior, design, and preparation for publishing by ActionWealthPublishing.Com

◆ *Introduction* ◆

Dedication

This book is dedicated to my father who prepared me to become a man from the age of five, and even though we parted so early, I was ready to take care of myself from the age of 12 and become the person I am today. Love you, Dad, and thank you (RIP). And to my mother—thank you for always believing in me.

To my Africa family who gave me the licence to go out and discover a new world, as well as the freedom to keep trying different business ideas for so many years.

To all my friends who have dared to try something new and who have shown the courage to be different. To the child I once was, and to every adult I see who plays with ideas in a child-like spirit.

To my two beautiful daughters, Jonell Semaganda and Tamiya Semaganda, for inspiring me to write all of my books and make the world a better place for you: I love you very much.

♦ *Introduction* ♦

TABLE OF CONTENTS

INTRODUCTION	**XIII**
PART I: SELF-MASTERY	**1**
CHAPTER 1: DISCOVERING WHO YOU ARE	**2**
DEFINING SELF	3
BLURRED IDENTITY	4
WE ARE NOT THINGS	6
YOU ARE THE CEO (CHIEF EXECUTIVE OFFICER)	7
SELECTING YOUR CALLING	9
TAKING CHANCES	10
THE IMPORTANCE OF CHARACTER	13
WATCH YOUR ENVIRONMENT	16
COURAGE AND DETERMINED EFFORT	20
SEEKING SUCCESS	25
CHAPTER 2: DEFINING MY *REASONS*	**27**
CREATE A LIFE ROADMAP	27
TAKE ACTION	28
I KNEW MY CALLING	31
MAKE THE MOST OF AVAILABLE OPPORTUNITIES	33
ADDED VALUE	34
FOLLOWING OPPORTUNITIES	37
STOP AND EVALUATE	39
SELF EVALUATION EXERCISE: WHERE ARE YOU NOW?	41
CHAPTER 3: KNOW WHAT YOU WANT	**48**
FEELING VICTIMIZED	48

IDENTIFY WHAT YOU DON'T WANT	49
DO MORE THAN IS REQUIRED	51
LEARN MORE THAN IS REQUIRED	52
SUCCESS IS SELDOM ACCIDENTAL	54
CHAPTER 4: INVEST IN YOURSELF	**57**
FEELING POWERLESS	57
LEARNED BEHAVIOR CAN BE UNLEARNED	58
GO AS FAR AS POSSIBLE	59
SEE YOURSELF AS A WINNER	61
THE VALUE OF CORRECT HABITS	65
EDUCATION AS DISTINGUISHED FROM LEARNING	69
MENTAL HEALTH	74
FEED YOUR MIND	76
GROW A THINKING MIND	78
CHAPTER 5: OUTWARD IMPRESSION	**86**
PHYSICAL HEALTH	86
STRESS AND ANXIETY	89
PRESENTATION: LOOK SUCCESSFUL; ACT SUCCESSFUL	93
THINK LIKE A LEADER; ACT LIKE A LEADER; BE A LEADER	98
CHAPTER 6: REACH OUT TO OTHERS	**102**
KINDNESS CAN GO VIRAL	102
KINDNESS AS A SIGN OF WEAKNESS?	103
CONSUMED BY ALL THE TAKERS	104
VOLUNTEER YOUR TIME	107
MONETARY GIVING	110
TEACH YOUR CHILDREN ABOUT MONEY	111
NEVER TOO LATE	112

♦ *Introduction* ♦

CHAPTER 7: LEARN FROM OTHERS   113

LEARN FROM THE BEST   113
THE IMPORTANCE OF ASSOCIATION   117
CHARACTER AND LEADERSHIP EXERCISE   122
FIND FIVE PEOPLE: THREE LOCAL AND TWO
   INTERNATIONAL   123
BE OPEN TO NEW CONCEPTS AND NEW IDEAS   125
ASK LOTS OF QUESTIONS   127

PART II: BUSINESS MASTERY   133

CHAPTER 8: YOU ARE A BUSINESS   134

BECOME KNOWLEDGEABLE ABOUT BUSINESS   134
LEARN NEW SKILLS   137
UNDERSTAND WHAT MAKES A BUSINESS   138
BUSINESS SHOULD GIVE YOU LIFE—NOT TAKE THE LIFE
   YOU HAVE   139
REASONS WHY NOT TO PUT ALL EGGS IN ONE BASKET
  140
THE EXAMPLE OF RICHARD BRANSON   141
ACCELERATE THE PROCESS   142

CHAPTER 9: MAKING MONEY WITH INFORMATION PRODUCTS   144

THE INFORMATION AGE   144
BOOKS & E-BOOKS   145
AUDIO BOOKS   149
SPECIAL REPORT   150
POWERPOINT PRESENTATION   151
WEBINARS   152
ONE-DAY WORKSHOPS   153
AUDIO, DVDs AND HOME-STUDY COURSES   155
CONSULTING, COACHING, GROUP-MENTORING   156

For free personal and business development training programs visit www.actionwealthacademy.com

LICENSING	157
AFFILIATES/JOINT VENTURES	158
PROFESSIONAL SPEAKER	159
SPONSORSHIPS	160
UNLIMITED POSSIBILITIES	161
CHAPTER 10: MAKING MONEY ONLINE	**163**
A LEVEL PLAYING FIELD	163
HOW MUCH MONEY DO YOU WANT TO MAKE?	165
BUILDING RELATIONSHIPS	166
MARKET YOUR OWN PRODUCT	168
AFFILIATE MARKETING	169
How to Get Started	*171*
You Will Need a Domain Name	*173*
Blog/Website	*174*
Hosting Provider	*174*
Banner	*175*
Create a Killer Bonus	*176*
Opt-In Form	*176*
PopUp Domination	*177*
Joint Venture	*178*
Start Internetworking	*179*
Start Making Commission Checks	*180*
CPA (COST PER ACTION)	180
DIFFERENCE BETWEEN CPA AND AFFILIATE MARKETING	180
Networks to Get Started	*181*
Types of CPA Opportunities	*182*
MEDIA BUYS	184
SUMMARY	185

◆ *Introduction* ◆

CHAPTER 11: MAKING MONEY WITH BUSINESS SYSTEMS   187

SYSTEMS ALL AROUND US   188
FIND THE TIME BANDITS   190
WORK LESS, ACCOMPLISH MORE   193
DESIGN YOUR LIFE/BUSINESS SYSTEM   195
A TURNKEY BUSINESS USES SYSTEMS   196

CHAPTER 12: MAKING MONEY WITH REAL ESTATE   200

LEVERAGE IS THE KEY TO SUCCESS   204
LEVERAGE WITH OWNER FINANCE   206
WE DON'T MAKE LAND   207
SET A REAL ESTATE GOAL   208
CREATE A STRATEGY   211
READ LOCAL NEWS   215
SHORT-TERM VS. LONG-TERM INVESTMENT   216
TREAT THIS AS A BUSINESS   218
FIND A REAL ESTATE MENTOR   220
DO YOUR HOMEWORK   221
KNOW YOUR ATTITUDE TO RISK   222
DEVELOP A WINNER'S ATTITUDE   223
ANYONE CAN PURCHASE PROPERTY   224

CHAPTER 13: GROWING WEALTH AS AN INVESTOR   226

INVESTING IS FOR EVERYONE AND ANYONE   226
EDUCATE YOURSELF   227
TEACH YOUR CHILDREN   229
HAVE A VISION TO TAKE YOUR COMPANY TO THE STOCK EXCHANGE   231

For free personal and business development training programs visit www.actionwealthacademy.com

PART III: FINANCIAL MASTERY 234
CHAPTER 14: ASSET & PERSONAL PROTECTION 238

BETTER TO BE SAFE THAN SORRY	238
CREATING BUSINESS CREDIT	240
USING A LIVING TRUST	242
INSURANCE	246
Life Insurance:	247
Disability Insurance	247
Health Insurance	248
Critical-Illness Policy	248
Umbrella Policy	249

CHAPTER 15: TAXATION BENEFITS 251

CHAPTER 16: RETIREMENT 254

THE RETIREMENT CONCEPT	254
AND THEN IT CHANGED	255
RETIREMENT IN THE PRESENT	256

CHAPTER 17: EFFICIENT RECORD-KEEPING 258

STAY ON TOP OF FINANCIALS	258
EXAMINE YOUR PROGRESS	259
ARE YOU MAKING A PROFIT?	259
CHARACTERISTICS:	260
OBJECTIVES	261

CHAPTER 18: HOW TO MAKE YOUR MONEY WORK FOR YOU 263

WORKING HARDER AND LONGER IS NOT THE ANSWER 263

ABOUT THE AUTHOR 265

For free personal and business development training programs visit **www.actionwealthacademy.com**

♦ *Introduction* ♦

Acknowledgements

Developing this book has not been a single-handed effort. Many individuals and companies have helped to shape my experience, as well as the content throughout this book. To all of my former and current business partners, shareholders, employees, clients and students: thank you for your support.

I want to express my extreme gratitude to the following friends and associates, without whom I never would have had the opportunity to learn, grow and share my experiences.

Let me first of all thank God for the gifts and opportunity provided to me to live a very purpose-driven life, along with the strength to keep going.

To the late Jim Rohn—an absolute legend. You came into my life 16 years ago, and your teaching and friendship changed my life as a teenager. Your philosophies and teaching will live on forever. I miss you. Rest in Peace.

To my friend Mark Victor Hansen, *Chicken Soup for the Soul*: You are a true pioneer of publishing and business strategy, and you have been a great teacher as well as friend. Thank you for your support on the Africa project.

To my buddy Chip Cummings, Northwind International Corp.: You have travelled to support me in Europe and Africa for so many years. I thank you for everything.

To Les Brown, Mr. Motivator himself: from the first time I saw that very old VHS tape of you speaking, working together, and sharing a stage, you not only made me believe that it's all possible, but you also become a good friend. Thank you.

To my good friend Imran Khan in Dubai: Thank you for everything over the years, but most importantly for being a friend. Thank you.

Introduction

I have written this book because I want to share my life experiences in order to help other people achieve their dreams and aspirations in life. So many people are quick to believe that they are stuck in their situation, and that there is no hope for them to better their lot in life. If they try to step up and try new things, as soon as an obstacle appears or adverse circumstances arise, they give up and quit. They quit trying. They quit striving. They quit on their own dreams.

It's amazing to me the number of people around the world who are not happy with their present circumstances. They feel that they are trapped and have no way of getting free. Many live what is known as a *hamster-wheel* existence. Each day they do the same things over and over but no progress is made. A week goes by, then a month, and then another year and they are still in the same place, doing the very same things. All the while, life is passing them by. They see themselves stuck in a rut and with no way out. (It has been said that a rut is a grave with both ends kicked out. It can certainly be considered a grave where a person's dreams die.)

So why is this true? Why do so many people give up so easily and quit? While other people, in the face of almost insurmountable odds, push upward and onward, and achieve great things in life? What's the difference? What is it that makes some people go and others stop? I wanted to know those answers.

I was definitely in that category of someone who faced seemingly insurmountable odds in my life. If you had seen my childhood and what I was up against, you probably would have thought that I had little chance of ever accomplishing anything of worth in my life.

I was born in a small village in Uganda located forty miles away from the capital city of Kampala. Out of necessity, I learned to survive at a very young age. From the time I was five years old until I was about twelve, war raged in our area. I saw more

◆ *Introduction* ◆

devastation and killing than any young child should ever see.

Men would show up at our school to recruit students to join the army, and some of the kids who were older than I actually did join. It was a time of guerrilla warfare, and it was difficult to sort it all out. Many of the government soldiers resorted to killing anyone who was in their way. They maintained that those of us in the villages were hiding people who were fighting the guerrilla war.

When soldiers came, we ran into the bush and climbed up into the trees to watch them. I remember many times sleeping in the bush because it was too dangerous to return to my village.

Because of the war, it was almost impossible to live a normal life—to do business or grow our food. Not a most promising beginning for any person. These are odds that I faced as a child; even today, many children around the world still face similar circumstances.

Eventually a few other family members and I left the village. I knew early on that life in our village was not the life for me. I knew that I wanted more. I knew I wanted to *be* more. I wanted to achieve great things and make a difference in the world.

My lofty dreams and visions seemed almost ludicrous in light of my living conditions, but I'm here to say that no matter where you are, no matter your station in life, no matter what has come up against you, you can be all that you have ever dreamed of being. Your life **can count for something.** You **can make a difference in your world.** You **can be the success you have dreamed of** being.

I had a heartfelt longing to learn how I could make my life important and useful. I did learn how. And now, many years later, I have accomplished a great many things in my life, and seen a lot along the way. I am now able to make a difference in my world, and in the lives of others. *Now I want to help you.*

That is the impetus behind my creating the Action Wealth System and writing this book. I

♦ *Introduction* ♦

wanted to create a step-by-step formula to help people just like you, starting right where you are, that guides you through developing a plan to get you where you want to go. Along the way, I will show you the process that will help you get there.

These are processes, techniques, and strategies that I have used for years in my own life. They are proven. If they can work for me—who came out of the poorest of poor environments, where there appeared to be no hope of ever rising above my circumstances—then they definitely can work for you.

This book is divided into three distinct sections. Each section is equally crucial in your quest for success. Each one deserves your full attention and follow-through.

- *Part I—Self-Mastery: Be the Very Best You Can Be*
- *Part II—Business Mastery: Create Multiple Streams of Income*
- *Part III—Financial Mastery: Keep More of Your Money and Make It Work Hard For You*

~PART I~
SELF-MASTERY

Be the Very Best You Can Be

Chapter 1

Discovering Who You Are

There is a reason why you chose this book. You didn't choose it by accident. Something deep inside of you is hungry for more. And that does not necessarily mean, hungry for owning more *stuff*. Not simply, having more money or more things—although that could be a part of it. What you are looking for is more meaning, more fulfilment, a higher quality of life.

Perhaps you're weary of being and doing the same old things in your life year after year. Something deep inside tells you that you were destined for greater things, but you're just not sure exactly what that might be. Nor do you know exactly where to begin, or how to get where you want to go.

This first section that I call *Self Mastery* is all about you. Working on self and learning how to be the best *you* that you can be—this is the starting point. Everything else is for naught if you are not sure about who you are and what you want.

Through the years, I have worked with hundreds and thousands of people from all walks of life. I see people chasing after wealth only to eventually sabotage their efforts because of a character flaw that hasn't been dealt with. So let's put first things first.

Defining Self

I remember having a conversation with one of my business clients a few years ago. This client shared the story of a man he knew who seemed to have no life outside of his job. Let's call this person Ray. Ray had no hobbies, hardly any friends, and even when it was obvious that he needed time to rest and recuperate his energies, he stubbornly refused to do. Upon further investigation it was discovered that Ray, who was an intelligent man of good upbringing, for some reason felt helpless outside of the work place. That was his comfort zone, and he could not imagine a life without his job position.

Now, I don't know Ray, but listening to this man's story it became apparent that Ray was the kind of person who defines himself solely by the major roles that he plays in society and in life. For Ray it was his *job description*.

We hear this all the time: "I'm a doctor." "I'm a musician." "I'm a writer." "I'm an engineer." "I'm a housewife." And the list goes on.

Blurred Identity

It is very easy to fall into the trap of referring to ourselves as *things,* or getting our identity all tangled up in our careers, work, family roles or job titles. We seem to believe that we are what we do, and we define ourselves exclusively in terms of the character or characters we play in life. Doing this seriously limits our potential and may even lead to life trauma. It is what I refer to as the perfect recipe for disaster!

◆ Self-Mastery ◆

> *To be nobody but yourself in a world which is doing its best, night and day, to make you everybody else means to fight the hardest battle which any human being can fight; and never stop fighting.*
>
> —e. e. cummings

Think about it. What happens to your identity when that job or role ends, or changes so radically that you can no longer identify yourself with it?

What happens when your business goes bust and you are no longer the *CEO of the Year?*

What happens when you are suddenly divorced and have no one to call *husband* or *wife?*

What happens when retirement looms and you are no longer the *attorney,* or *engineer,* or *accountant?*

You often hear about people who at a certain point in life—usually in mid-life—suddenly begin to question what they have come to believe about themselves. It happens every day. Some even have a name for this experience. They call it the *mid-life crisis*.

A perfect example is when recession hits our nation and global economies, and an *executive* loses his or her six-figure income. Or the *finance guy* has to give up the company car and all the perks and benefits that come with his job because their employer is bought out or goes bankrupt.

What of the parents who never looked outside their roles as mom or dad, and found themselves depressed "old roosters" when the kids left home?

It's never easy for such people to deal with these drastic changes, especially if they have spent years defining themselves *only* by the things that they do.

We Are Not Things

The truth is, *we are not things*. It is very easy to use labels to describe ourselves or define other people. "Oh, I'm an accounts clerk." Or, "He's my lawyer." Or, "She's a flight attendant." Even innocent descriptions such as "I'm a Christian" or "a Muslim," "a Democrat" or "a Republican" are effortlessly used to define ourselves all the time, despite these same descriptions in themselves being seriously self-limiting.

We are not our jobs, our roles, our positions in society, our bank balances, or any of a thousand other possible partial descriptors we may want to use.

I do not dispute the fact that, by doing what we do every day, we become much a part of them as they become of us. But we must always bear in mind that we are *not things*. We are human *beings* and not human *doings*. We need to be constantly reminded to see ourselves and others in much larger and more *alive* terms. By doing this we have a better chance of truly finding ourselves.

You Are the CEO (Chief Executive Officer)

Throughout this book about wealth creation and building your success-filled life, we will be talking a great deal about you taking control. It is now time for you to take responsibility for your own life. You are the CEO and chairman of your own company. You may be thinking, *What company? I'm not head of any company.*

I am encouraging you to think of your own life as your own company. This is the company I am referring to. And you definitely are the person in charge. There is absolutely no reason why you shouldn't take charge of your own life. Sometimes you may need to be reminded that this is *your* life. You know what is best for you, and that means you are the best person to be at the helm.

In the seminars and conferences that I present, I tell the attendees that they are each one a CEO and chairman of their own company. I get a lot of surprised looks, and looks of doubt as well.

Then I tell them that your *name* is your company. You must be the CEO of your own company because the fact of the matter is, you are the only one who should decide what you do and how you will do it.

Selecting Your Calling

There are things you know that others do not know. You have skills and abilities that you enjoy doing. It may be something that you are good at doing and love to do have never had the time or the opportunity. Or perhaps it's your *hobby*. (Later in the book you will learn how you can turn your hobby into an income stream.)

Take time to ask yourself what it is that you *really truly* want. This is where it all begins. Most people will say they want good health, and at the same time they want enough money to do what they want to do and when they want to do it. Those are certainly not bad things to want to have in life. But it's time to be more specific. Think about what you can offer the world. What can you do that will make a difference and will help others?

Do you want to just *make a living*, or would you rather create a good life? A fulfilling life. A life that will make a difference for the world around you. It's your decision.

It would be a good thing to actually write a list of some of your highest desires in life. Be specific. Set realistic, attainable goals. Where would you like to be this time next year? Two years from now? Five years from now. Begin to visualize yourself in that place. See yourself doing the things you long to do. Being the person you long to be.

As this book progresses, you will learn more methods whereby you can achieve these goals.

Taking Chances

As I disclosed in the introduction, my childhood days were filled with fear and danger. In a way, the wars worked to my advantage because the unrest in our area drove me to take a huge risk.

It happened when I was about nine years old. I became restless and frustrated living in our small village. We were continually moving to ensure our safety which added to my sense of frustration. Even at that young age, I knew I wanted more. I wasn't sure what *more* consisted of, but I knew that I had to leave. I was weary of the responsibility I was required to carry. I did not want to be the man of the house anymore. I wanted to strike out on my own, to go somewhere, but I didn't know where. I had no concrete plan, but I knew I had to do something.

While we were living with one of my aunts, I became friends with the men who drove the charcoal truck that came from town to collect charcoal from our village twice a week and then deliver it into Kampala. By becoming friends with these men I learned that it was my own uncle who was the mechanic that repaired their truck. I further learned that one of my cousins who had left the village served as an apprentice to my uncle. There was no mechanic's shop as such: they simply repaired cars in the street.

All of this started me to thinking. I reasoned that, if my cousin could leave the village, I could do the same. I knew if my mother or my aunt knew of my plans, however, they would try to stop me, so I told no one.

One night when the men were in our village, I waited until after dark and then hid in the back of their truck. If they found me later I reasoned, since they were my friends, I knew they wouldn't just leave me by the side of the road. But if I told them ahead of time, I was sure they wouldn't let me go.

I was right. By the time they found me, they were willing to take me right to where my uncle lived. That decision changed the course of my life. It opened up a whole new world for me.

At nine years of age, I knew I had to take a chance. I had to step out and make a difference in my own life. I couldn't sit around waiting for things to happen. It's the same for you. Taking chances is not a bad thing—that is, unless you are taking foolish uncalculated risks. Then it can be dangerous.

At some point you must shift over from dreaming and planning to actually taking action. You will have to move out of your comfort zone and learn to do new things. That's exactly what I did.

♦ *Self-Mastery* ♦

The Importance of Character

It has been said that *character is what you do when no one else is looking*. Character is your own decision to be a person of honor and integrity. To be a person of your word; a person who can be counted on. Your character will be the very foundation upon which you build your life.

If I were to present a full list of essential character traits it would be quite lengthy, but let's look at some of the more basic ones:

- Trustworthiness
- Respect
- Responsibility
- Fairness
- Caring
- Citizenship

Check to see if, within any of these areas of basic character traits, you are found lacking. Are there areas in which you need work?

When I arrived in Kampala, I discovered that my uncle lived in a very small place and had no room for me. I was fine with that since I was accustomed to sleeping in the bush. I just made my bed in a nearby shed. When he was ready to go to work the next day, I asked to go along, telling him that I could be of help. Of course he wasn't sure at first. After all, I was just a skinny little kid.

My uncle worked on petrol cars and cars with carburettors—they didn't have injectors as they do now. Within three months, I could take an engine apart and put it back together. I became really good because I was on a mission. I knew that I had to be better than the other kids or else my uncle might send me back to the village.

It worked. Very soon he stopped even thinking about sending me away because he knew that I was very useful to him. He could send me somewhere to do work for him and then he received all the money. In fact, when my father came looking for me to take me back to return to school, my uncle told him he hadn't seen me! My good character was all working in my favour.

The importance of character can affect an entire nation. At the end of World War II, Japan was a nation that stood in overwhelming need of assistance to recover from a war that left her an empty shell. Therefore, for Japanese citizens to be able to fill this emptiness and once again lead normal lives in a world without war, it was necessary for its government to introduce a radical educational program. This program focused on teaching Japan's children the value of a positive attitude, honesty, integrity, and enthusiasm. The goal was that they experience a firm foundation to assist them in tackling issues in the real world. It was this positive and motivating teaching of good character that brought a war-ravaged nation out of destruction and into prosperity.

Having an impeccable character is crucial to achieving lasting success in your life. By beginning with self to achieve success, make sure that building strong character is part of your plan.

Watch Your Environment

Do you spend time with small thinkers? Do you listen to all the naysayers who belittle your dreams and aspirations? Do you allow negative people to influence your plans and your actions? If so, it's time to break out of those associations.

This is why I chose not to disclose my plan to leave the village to anyone. I kept it to myself because I couldn't take the chance that someone might talk me out of it, or accuse me of being foolhardy. I had to listen to my own heart and go with that.

So whatever you do, think big. I always say: *learn to think for yourself, but if you're going to think at all, think BIG.* If you're thinking about conquering your city, why not go for your country?!

Donald Trump, fondly referred to as "The Donald," is one such man who is definitely a big thinker. In his book *Why We Want You to Be Rich*, co-authored with Robert Kiyosaki, he says this: "Let's not just think big. Let's think expansively and this includes seeing what is possible, and making 'it' happen." You can tell that Mr. Trump thinks expansively. All you have to do is visit New York City and count the skyscrapers bearing his name to know that this is true.

In yet another example, there's good reason why renowned neurosurgeon Ben Carson, MD, dedicated an entire book to the idea of thinking big. (See *Think Big* by Ben Carson.) Awarded the Presidential Medal of Freedom, the highest civilian honour possible, on June 19, 2008 by former President George W. Bush for his work and impact, Dr. Carson achieved big dreams and continues to impact the lives of hundreds of American youth. This is primarily because he learned very early the significance of thinking BIG.

Ben Carson grew up in the poorer section of Detroit, Michigan. His parents were divorced which meant that his mother was gone a great deal of the time, working two and three jobs to support her two sons. She encouraged her boys to turn off the television and read books. It changed Ben's life. He went from the bottom of his fifth grade class to the top of his sixth grade class in one and a half years.

With his mother's support and constant encouragement, he began to dream big dreams.

Later in his life, he earned a scholarship to Yale and became the head of pediatric neurosurgery at Johns Hopkins Hospital when he was thirty-three years old. He went on to become the first neurosurgeon to ever separate twins who were conjoined at the head.

Dr. Carson's life points out the fact that when you dream big, you not only affect your own life, but the lives of many others, as well. It would be impossible to measure the gratitude of families around the world who have benefitted from this doctor's dedication and expertise.

Nelson Mandela, who led South Africa from apartheid to democracy, was an eloquent and inspirational figure who advocated for peace, democracy and human rights throughout his entire life. Although born in a humble village into an early life that he described as dominated by "custom, ritual and taboo," and where he spent his time as a young boy tending to herds of cattle like so many other African children, he nevertheless dreamed of freedom and leadership. "One day I will be the first black president of South Africa," he said in 1952, even though this was a wildly improbable idea and far from his life at the time, being arrested for ANC activities opposing apartheid.

Throughout even his later imprisonment, Nelson Mandela refused to negotiate for his release on the condition that he renounce his protests against the apartheid government because he had one big, seemingly impossible, dream in his mind. To him, accepting anything less simply was not an option. His legacy reminds us that our dreams, like his, should be almost bigger than we can imagine. But by dreaming big, we can program our brain to the possibilities, and inspire ourselves to find ways to get what we want.

When I speak to audiences, I remind them that when they set goals, everything depends on a good start, a bit of motivation, and the right road. *"A careful preparation is half the battle won."* Meaning if you start your pursuit of any goal on the right footing, you will most definitely find your way to the end.

Part of that right footing is take careful attention to the environment in which you find yourself. Choose to spend time with those who are doing what you are dreaming of doing. Listen to them; learn from them. (More on this subject later in the book.) Refuse to hang around with losers who are going nowhere.

Courage and Determined Effort

Another important success factor in your life is courage. How are you doing in the area of courage? Do you see yourself as an individual who can step out and make things happen? Or do you entertain a dream and, in the next second, shoot it down because of some fear of leaving your comfort zone?

The forceful, energetic character, like the forceful soldier on the battle-field, not only moves forward to victory himself, but his example has a stimulating influence on others. The zealous, energetic man unconsciously carries others along with him. His example is contagious and compels imitation.

> *We all have defining moments. It is in these moments that we find our true characters. We become heroes or cowards; truth tellers or liars; we go forward or backward.*
>
> —Robert Kiyosaki

The beginner who is studying success should carefully examine the lives of men and women whose undaunted courage has won in the face of obstacles that would deter weaker natures. And what goes with courage? I call it *effort*. It has been truly said that to *desire to possess without being burdened by the trouble of acquiring is simple naiveté*. Even leisure cannot be enjoyed unless it is won by effort. The Bible reminds us that he who does not toil for his bread must not eat.

I don't believe that it is possible for an unemployed person, however amiable and otherwise respectable, to ever be really happy. So I always find it surprising to walk up to a young man or woman and ask them what it is that they do, and they happily respond "nothing" or that they "cannot find anything to do."

Is it really possible to be content doing nothing? Is it okay for there to be nothing to do? Or is it that we are breeding a generation of lazy yearlings who look for excuses to do nothing?

Surely it could not have been sheer boredom on the part of our Creator that He created work to be for us a necessary evil in our lives. Work was His design in the first place. So, if you have nothing to do then, by the same token, expect nothing out of life. No excuses!

The world is full of so many opportunities. They are available for everyone alike, and just waiting to be grabbed. A world full of opportunity cannot be taken, however, by your living in fear and cowardice; rather it requires a great deal of courage.

Courage is when you feel tired but you still decide to get your work done. Courage is when you haven't slept enough the night before and it's cold outside, and you really just feel like staying in and getting some extra sleep, yet you still get yourself out of bed, go to the gym and work out because you made a fitness commitment.

Courage is when you have tried several business ideas and ventures without any success yet, instead of giving up, you hang in there knowing that you are getting closer and closer to success. Courage is when you get out of your comfort zone to learn a new skill or try a new fun activity without worrying about looking like a fool. Courage is when you live your life and get hurt or make bad decisions, but you get right back up and move on.

For most of us, we might experience many roadblocks to success along with self-defeating tendencies. Whether it's fear or insecurities or caring what others think, we end up becoming our own worst enemies. Yet the world is there for the taking.

A great example of courage was exhibited by Martin Luther King, Jr., whose dream was to see an America with racial equality for all citizens, no matter their colour or race. He not only overcame the prejudices of the times in which he lived, but, with determined effort, he brought home this truth to his countrymen. With Mr. King's type of courage and determined effort applied in <u>your</u> daily life, how could it not be possible to achieve everything you want?

Few think of the late Nelson Mandela without remembering the extraordinary courage it took him to endure those 27 years, most in a tiny cell at Robben Island, and to persist in his faith that ending apartheid was as essential for his countrymen and women as food and breath. In fact, in spite of all that he had to endure, former President Mandela often wrote eloquently about courage, itself. He said:

"I learned that courage was not the absence of fear, but the triumph over it. The brave man is not he who does not feel afraid, but he who conquers that fear."

It takes tremendous courage to take the entrepreneurial risks necessary to become wealthy. It takes courage to step out of your comfort zone. It takes courage to take honest stock of where you are and where you want to be. It takes courage to fire your boss. It takes courage to be courageous!

Seeking Success

Success is not an end but a work-in-progress. Even as you achieve greater and greater heights, your growth should never really end. Over the past 15 or so years, I have lived a life based on a number of philosophies, one of them being: *"Whatever your hand finds to do, do with all your might"* Ecclesiastes 9:10.

Is this what success is all about—doing all you can to the best of your ability no matter what?

There are a great number of paths the observant young man can see before him; question is, which of these paths shall he wisely pursue that will lead him ending in victory?

It was Sir Winston Churchill who said: *"Success is moving from failure to failure without losing enthusiasm."*

But how do I begin to fail if I cannot identify what my hands can do? And how can I win? Who will tell me the work for which I am best fitted? Where is that kind guide who will point out the life-path that will lead me to success?

In Chapter 2, you will learn why it's important to know your reasons for doing what you are doing. You must know what it is that motivates you.

Chapter 2

Defining My *Reasons*

Create a Life Roadmap

To find yourself, you must define your reasons. This is the process that every individual must go through who aims to discovers his or her life purpose. What is it that you <u>really</u> want to do, and do you have a plan of action for it? What are your reasons for being? What drives you? Where do you see yourself in a couple of years? In five years? What is your true calling?

Many of us are members of a wandering generation. We are just travelling from point A to point B and hoping to find our way to the next pit-stop at point C—wherever and whenever that may be. We make no effort or attempt to plan our directions.

Defining your reasons and creating a life road map is one of those tasks that, if not performed well from the outset, often leads to unnecessary misgivings later on in life. You will end up spending most of your years doing something someone else thought would fit you, or because it was the most convenient thing to do and there was nothing else available for you to do. (Or so it seemed at the time.) Maybe you simply walked into a job for no reason, not asking yourself if it was the right thing for you. This is not the best route to take to find who you really are. However, if this is where you now find yourself, don't despair, because you can still be the agent of change for your own life.

Take Action

In the process of discovering your true calling, you cannot stand hesitating and doubting too long. I know of a young man who used to attend my speaking seminars and each time at the end of the sessions he would walk up to me, seeking advice on what to do with his life. I barely knew the guy, but

◆ *Self-Mastery* ◆

from the little he shared with me I could see that here was a young man full of potential. However, he was spending his life worrying about his future or lack of it.

I remember at the end of one success seminar where I had been speaking about how the youth can gain work experience by doing volunteer work, he walked up to me as he usually did, and shook my hand vigorously. He seemed more upbeat than usual and said he had always thought of doing volunteer work but was not sure whether it was the right thing to do; he had been thinking about it for the last year or so.

I was astonished and surprised that someone so young and so smart could sit for months mulling over whether or not it was the right thing to do—working for nothing while gaining real experience that was bound to benefit him in the long run. What was there to consider?

In my opinion there are some things worth thinking about and those not worth losing your sleep over, especially if they fall in the category of common sense.

Anyway, the young man was now willing to try his hand at volunteering, seeing that he had had no luck finding paying work. He soon joined a not-for-profit organization, and eleven months later I received an email from him informing me that he had just been offered a permanent position within the organization where he had been volunteering. He was now actively involved in doing exactly what he'd always aspired to do.

My point? Stop thinking and mulling things over in your mind! Enter somewhere and do it *now*. Take Action! No matter how hard or disagreeable the work, do it with all your might. The effort will strengthen you and qualify you to find work in future that is more in accord with your calling.

> *"Discipline yourself to do the things you need to do when you need to do them, and the day will come when you will be able to do the things you want to do when you want to do them."*

◆ *Self-Mastery* ◆

—Zig Ziglar

I Knew My Calling

As I mentioned in the last chapter, my early years were fill with memories of war and killing. I definitely knew what my calling (my reason) was at that early age. It was clear, specific, and simple: *Find a way to survive.*

War was raging through the villages where we lived, and the unrest forced us to move to another part of the country where it was safe enough for us kids to go to school. However we did not have any money to buy food. Decisions had to be made as to how to feed our family. It was suggested that I be the one to go to the nearest trading centre to buy merchandise wholesale, and then sell items retail to the villagers. Whatever profit I made would then be used for our basic survival.

Amidst a raging war in a small village in an obscure part of Uganda, I came to understand that this was the only way possible to feed the hungry mouths of both my immediate and my extended families. I had no way of knowing how long this would be the case. It was very difficult at my age to bear such a weight; however, as soon as I experienced the *high* that comes with undertaking a *profit-making venture*, and as soon as I understood the concept of buying low and selling high, I knew that this was something I was willing to do long-term.

Living in the village and balancing school and family chores while constantly shifting from place to place did not make this new vocation an easy one. After a few months, the war subsided and we went back home. But I was reluctant. I did not want to go back to our old village life. Living there meant constantly tending to the coffee plantation, daily treks twice a day to fetch water from the stream, and going back to my village school. It was a heavy load. What's more, my dad realized that I had grown some, and so he took me under his wing to pass on to me the responsibility of buying and selling of coffee. I had literally become the man to earn my own money for things I needed, forfeiting early on the joys of being a carefree child.

My responsibility was to carry heavy loads of coffee beans from one end of the garden to the other, and lay them out in the sun to dry. Later, as the sun set, I had to hurriedly pack the dried beans in sisal bags before my dad came home to inspect the day's activities. I lived in a constant state of exhaustion. This was the point in my young life that I made the decision to leave when I got a chance.

Make the Most of Available Opportunities

On your search to finding your calling, it is important to make the most of every opportunity that comes your way (it could very well be your last). I call this being *useful*. If you are useful, then those around you will help you, knowingly or unknowingly, along your search for whatever it is you are looking for. Successful people are successful because they add value to the marketplace.

Bill Gates is the man he is today not because he had the brains of Einstein, but because of the company he built. Microsoft has decidedly changed the way in which the world functions. Of course, it helped that Gates was a geek who loved electronic gadgets, but there's no doubt that the world is a better place *with* computers than it was *without* them.

One could argue that the computer revolution would have happened even without Gates, but the reality is that more than 90% of the world's computers run Microsoft's Windows. He developed his machines and built his company step by step, and through being useful, he managed to have tremendous impact on society by adding value to our lives.

Added Value

So very simply, success can be equated to added value. By adding value you make the world a better place. How can you add value? Simple. By serving others, which I refer to as being useful.

"If you help other people get what they want, those people will help you get what you want."

—Zig Ziglar

Life in the city was somewhat exciting for me. I couldn't speak a single word of English, but I knew and understood implicitly that I had to somehow ensure my permanent residency in town or be taken back to the village.

I was just a month shy of thirteen years old when I ran away from home. My primary occupation became learning my way around my uncle's auto mechanic business and trying to be as useful as possible.

I was forever running around with a spanner (wrench) in my hand, ducking under greasy car bonnets or looking at car wiring, trying to earn my way. Very quickly I learned a great deal about cars, and my uncle began to *value* my presence at the garage. However, because I was very small in stature, I was unable to do the heavier jobs such as lifting the gear box or a car engine, for example. Because of this, I knew my days at the garage were numbered.

Following Opportunities

Three months later (when I was still in fear of being sent away or my dad finally locating me), a young guy came to the garage riding a moped (small motorcycle). He looked too young to own such a nice moped, so I asked him how did he manage to buy it, and he joked by saying that I should go work with him.

He was joking and didn't realize that I was not the type of a kid you joke with. I found out where he worked, showed up at 7AM, and waited for him there. He was shocked to see me and told me that he didn't have anything for me to do. But I told him that I was really good at making myself useful. If I could watch him for a day and get to understand what he did, I was sure that I could find something to help him with.

I left the garage and went to work for that younger man who was only a few years older than I was. Not only did he own his own moped, but he ran a cosmetics shop in the heart of Kampala. Even though I knew little about him, I knew that I had a better chance at surviving and earning my own way with him—far away from my uncle's garage.

As I had done at the garage, I quickly learned everything about the cosmetics shop. Within a very short time I was selling more cosmetics than had ever been sold at the shop before I arrived. Not only did I add immense value to this man's business, but to my relief I avoided getting myself fired and losing any chance I had to eventually start my own business.

Learning to be useful and learning to bring value to others are what provided me countless opportunities thereafter. Remember this important concept and it will serve you well in life.

Barely a teenager, I had a clearly defined reason: SURVIVAL.

And because I was always trying to find a way to survive (number #1 reason), I learned to become useful (add value) and, as a result, learned how to make a profit (success).

REASON + VALUE = SUCCESS

Stop and Evaluate

Now that you've read this far, and now that you realize it's time to discover who you are, to define your *reason,* and to become really useful in some area, it's <u>time to take action.</u>

The action I'm referring to actually means that you must *stop* for a time and evaluate. Throughout this book, you will find a set of questions and exercises for you to complete. These are not tacked on as an afterthought; rather they are the real warp and woof of this entire book. It requires something from you. It requires your time, thought, and attention. Obviously, if you are determined to make your own personal choice for success, you will have no qualms about this requirement. Nor about investing the needed time.

What you will need to get started is a block of uninterrupted quiet time. You will need a private place. You will need to be alone, with pencil and paper in hand. You will need to be as focused as possible. Turn off your cell phone and your computer.

(And the iPad and iPod, as well!) Minimize distractions as much as possible.

I encourage you to not think of this as a one-time event. Instead, begin to see these times of brainstorming as vital and necessary to your advancement in life. Too much of your life is now being spent in mindless activities. That's why the *hamster wheel* way of living is so frustrating for you—it demands so little of you. You need a challenge to awaken your inner creativity.

If finding a time of quiet is difficult for you, call a family meeting. Explain to the other members of your family that you need to do a little soul-searching, and politely request the amount of quiet time that you need. You may be surprised at how willing your family members are to cooperate with you, once they are aware of your needs. (Too often we expect that those close to us will second-guess our needs. This is seldom effective. Open communication always works best.)

Now that you have selected the time and place, and you are focused, it's time to tackle the following questions:

Self Evaluation Exercise: WHERE ARE YOU NOW?

Answer the following questions as honestly as possible.

1) Write down 5 words that best describe YOU (e.g. Funny intelligent, determined, etc.)

   a) _____

   b) _____

   c) _____

   d) _____

   e) _____

♦ Action Wealth System ♦

2. Write down 5 things that you would like to achieve in the next 6 months.

   a) _____

   b) _____

   c) _____

   d) _____

   e) _____

3. On a scale of 0%–100%, how would you rate yourself in terms of:

   a) **Your ability to make money?**
   <Where: 0 % = You are not capable of making any money; 50% = You are earning the "average" income in your community; 100% = You are earning all the money you could possibly want to use or want.>

   Your rate % _____

b) **Your ability to get along with others (outside your family)** <Where 0 % = You can't get along with anybody for a length of time; nobody likes you; 50% = You are reasonably well liked; 100% = You are universally loved, admired and respected by everyone you meet.>

Your rate % _____

c) **Your ability to get along with your family**? <Where 0 % = You are totally unable to get along with your family; 50% = You have less friction, fights. You get along better with your family than most of the people you know; 100% = Your relationships with your family group is so outstanding that you potentially may be selected by some civic group as the "best of the year.">

Your rate % _____

d) **Your capabilities as a leader?**
<Where: 0 % = You can't remember a single time when others did anything you suggested. You never get your way in a group activity; 50% = About half the time

you find yourself guiding or leading the way in group activities; 100% = Wherever you go, whatever you do, you're always the person others look toward for leadership. If there's an election at work, in a club or group. You're picked to run things.>

Your rate % _____

e) **Your work skills?** <Where: 0 % = You are totally unable to get along with your family; 50% = You are no better or worse than most other people you know doing the same job; 100% = You are better at your job than anyone else you know or have heard about.>

Your rate % _____

f) **Your power of persuasion?** <Where: 0 % = You can't remember ever having talked anyone into doing anything they didn't want to do; 50% = You are not especially persuasive when you try to convince others, but you are now otherwise at this than most of the people you know; 100% =

◆ *Self-Mastery* ◆

You could sell an electric fan to an Eskimo.>

Your rate % _____

g) **Your Sport or Hobby activities?** <Where: 0 % = You don't excel in sports at all. Your hobbies or projects are total flops; 50% = You have never reached that level of skill which represents the average. Half the people you know are better than you in this regard. Half do not do as well nor score as high; 100% = At your favourite sport or hobby activity, you perform at a professional level good enough to compete with champions, without handicap.>

Your rate % _____

h) **How lucky you are?** < Where: 0 % = If there is a way for something to go wrong it will; 50% = You get as many breaks as most people do; 100% = You are always a winner. Luck is your best friend.>

Your rate % _____

♦ Action Wealth System ♦

i) **How smart you are?** <Where: 0 % = Not smart at all; 50% = No smarter nor dumber than most; 100% = There is no one nor anything that is yet to fool you.>

Your rate % _____

j) **How others see you?** <Where: 0 % = You are convinced that everyone looks down on you; 50% = People consider you "average"; 100% = Everyone looks up to you and thinks you are superior

k) **If you lost your job today, how easy would it be for you to pick yourself up and move on?** <Where: 0% = Not a chance; 50% = 50 / 50 chance; 100% = Very easy.>

Your rate % _____

TOTAL SCORE _____

MEAN SCORE _____ (Total Score divided by number of questions)

For free personal and business development training programs visit www.actionwealthacademy.com

MEAN SCORE = SELF IMAGE

The way you answer these questions will affect the way you behave, interact with others, and react to situations. It is very important that you avoid defining yourself as anything negative. Simply think of what type of person you aspire to be and start defining yourself as that type of person.

With each step that you progress through in this book, you are gaining knowledge about yourself and your future. In the next chapter, you will gain more clarity about exactly what it is that you want your life to look like.

Chapter 3

Know What You Want

Feeling Victimized

In Chapter 1, we talked about finding your own calling in life. For many people this is a totally foreign concept. To think that they actually have a choice in the direction of their life seldom if ever occurs to them. They are stuck in a lifestyle that holds no promise of fulfillment. Their existence is a robotic repetition of doing the same thing day after day. They feel trapped with no way out.

Such existence can cause a person to feel victimized.

Thoughts go through their mind such as:

> ➢ *Nothing good ever happens for me*

- ➤ I get all the bad luck
- ➤ Other people get all the breaks
- ➤ My boss doesn't like me; I'll never get a promotion
- ➤ I don't have the inside track that so-and-so has
- ➤ It's not what you know, it's who you know, and I just don't know the right people

Victim thinking is a sure way to stay stuck in the rut that I referred to in the introduction. As long as the blame is placed on circumstances and other people, no progress toward true success will ever be made. Nothing will ever change. It's when you finally decide that it's in your power to take control of your life that the changes will come.

Identify What You Don't Want

If you're still not exactly sure what you want to do with your life, it may be enough just to know what you *don't* want. (In *Part II*, you will learn a few strategies for how to begin to create streams of income so that you no longer feel stuck in a place of employment that you don't like.)

When I began working for my uncle, I essentially made myself of great value to him. He knew he could count on me, and he saw that I learned quickly and easily. But was I happy? Not at all. As I said previously, there was no shop. We worked outside on the streets in all kinds of weather. The rainy times were the worst. I didn't like the grease and lying underneath vehicles on the dirty street. I grew weary of always being dirty.

At the time, I still didn't know what I wanted, but I was becoming more aware of what I *didn't* want. And I knew that I didn't want to be a mechanic.

What are the things in your life that make you feel unfulfilled? Is it an empty, dead-end job? Is it the sadness you feel at having missed past opportunities? Is it the fact that other people seem to be more in control of your life than you are?

As you allow yourself to once again pursue your dreams and aspiration, you will become more and more aware of what you *don't want* in your life.

Do More Than is Required

In Chapter 1 you learned that you are the CEO of your own company. This is true even if you are trapped in a dead-end job with a boss who is less than nice to you. Once you create a paradigm shift, once you begin to see yourself in control of your life, you will behave differently. You are no longer working for the company that hands you your paycheck. You are working for *you*. No longer do you see yourself caught in the hamster-wheel life. You are on your way up and out. This means that you can go the extra mile; do more than is required. You may be surprised at the results.

When I worked as a mechanic for my uncle, there was really no need for me to learn how to take an entire engine apart. But I did it anyway. I did more than was required. That established a pattern in my life that extends to this very day. No matter what I'm doing, I make it a point to go the extra mile. In business this is known as "under-promise and over-deliver." Doing more than is required will hold you in good stead no matter what you're doing.

Once you see yourself as being CEO of your own company, you will cease to think of yourself as a victim. You will move from being a <u>victim</u> to becoming a <u>victor</u> in your life.

Learn More Than is Required

We will talk more later in the book about life-long learning, but for now it's sufficient to point out that the more you learn, the better equipped you are to take control of your life and become the wealth-builder that you dream of being.

Henry Ford once said, "*Anyone who stops learning is old, whether at twenty or eighty. Anyone who keeps learning stays young. The greatest thing in life is to keep your mind young.*" This is even more true now than it was when Henry Ford said it.

We are living in the *information age*, which means that no matter what field or industry you are involved in, you must continually learn to stay abreast of all that is going on. There is a type of learning that's known as *maintenance* learning—which means, you are keeping up with what's going on. This is good, but in our day and age, it will not be enough.

Another type of learning is known as *growth* learning. This is when you are adventurous enough to learn a brand new skill. Something you've never tried before. The learning curve may be steep, but you are up to the challenge. For instance, let's say you want to learn more about earning money online. There are many ways to do this, and in order to know how to do it efficiently and effectively, you will have to learn a new skill set.

Growth learning will always be mind-expanding. You will find yourself doing things that you never did before, and because of that your self-confidence will grow stronger.

Since knowledge is one of the major sources of value in today's culture, your capacity to expand your mind and give yourself over to lifelong learning will break many of the success barriers that seem to be stopping you. Make it a point to set aside time for ongoing education in your life.

Success Is Seldom Accidental

My recipe to success is very simple: decide what you want, find someone who does it the best, and do what they do. I have improved upon it by saying, find *five* people who are the very best at doing what you want to do and study *them*. Successful people always have documentation about how they started and got to where they are. Take advantage and read about them.

The people in the world who you know to be successful in their given field did not get to where they are by chance or happenstance. It's no accident that they have made great achievements in their lives. Those who are living the lives of their dreams have

♦ Self-Mastery ♦

ventured out of their comfort zone and dared to do what others will not do.

Who is it that you admire? Is it someone like Richard Branson of Virgin Group? Or Mark Zuckerberg, founder of Facebook? Or maybe Jack Canfield, the originator of the *Chicken Soup for the Soul* series? With more than 500 million books in print, and having given rise to an entirely new genre in literature, Jack is highly qualified to talk about and teach success principles.

Or perhaps one of your heroes is someone like real estate mogul Barbara Corcoran, who took a $1,000 loan and turned it into a real estate business—a business that she later sold for $66 million. You may even admire someone who is lesser known, such as American entrepreneur Corey T. Nyman, who started a business in Oregon called *Labor Wines*. Nyman is someone who is living his dream. For more than a decade, he fantasized about making and selling his own Oregon wine, and now that dream is a reality. Up against amazing odds, he did not quit and built a company that believes that hard work presents rewards. While his production is small at this time, thanks the owner's vision and persistence, Labor Wine is available in more than 35 states, "from their hands t o yours."

No matter who it is that you admire and want to emulate, I encourage you to find and read their biographies. Learn about these peoples' lives. explore how they faced and overcame obstacles. You will quickly come to realize that they are no different than you. They did not have special favors from a rich relative. They didn't know all the right people. They pushed through because they had a *vision* and they had a *passion*. Then, they dared to follow that vision and that passion

Your success will depend entirely upon your drive and your desire and your willingness to get back up when you get knocked down.

Success is not an accident.

Chapter 4

Invest in Yourself

Feeling Powerless

As has been mentioned, I encourage you to think of your life as your own company. Why is this so important? It's important because only you know the dreams and aspirations that *you* entertain in your mind and subconscious. Only you can set things in motion so that they can come to pass.

One of the reasons that people remain locked in a dead-end, unfulfilling lifestyle is because they see themselves as powerless. This, as was pointed out earlier, is known as a *victim mentality*. The feeling of being powerless, being victimized, is something that a person learns through the course of their life when their basic childhood needs were not met. When the needs are not met, a sense of low self-esteem results.

This negative thinking leads the person to believe that other people and outside circumstances are responsible for all the problems and shortcomings they experience. One of the characterizations of a victim mentality is an attitude of blaming others and complaining about existing conditions.

Learned Behavior Can Be Unlearned

The good news is that, because this is a *learned behavior,* it can also be *unlearned.* You don't have to live in that pattern anymore. Past experiences may have led you to believe negative things about yourself. In fact, these core beliefs may be part of what has you trapped in the rut that you are in. (That rut that you are longing to be set free from.)

One of the first steps is to acknowledge your victim thinking. See it for what it really is and step into your new role of taking responsibility. Learn to appreciate the unique person that you are; appreciate your gifts, talents and abilities. Become confident in the person you are, that you are capable and competent. Remind yourself that you are the CEO of your own private company. As such, you must conduct yourself in a manner fitting of this position.

When you make mistakes or fall short of the goals that you've set, forgive yourself. Learn to become your own ally; your own friend. The more you learn to respect yourself, the more others will respect you as well. The more you learn to respect yourself, the more freedom you will feel to move out of your comfort zone.

As you begin to change your thinking about who you are and what you can accomplish, you will have no more time to spend blaming or complaining. You will be too busy building your new life.

Go As Far As Possible

In Chapter 1, I gave examples of successful people who were not afraid to think big. Who would have ever thought that a young African-American boy from a poor neighborhood in Detroit, MI—a boy who was last in academics in his fifth-grade class—would become a world-renowned brain surgeon? It seemed virtually impossible.

What does your background look like? For that matter what does your present life look like? Does it seem like you have every strike against you? It's time to realize that none of that matters. What matters is that you *believe in you*, and that you are willing to do what it takes to change your circumstances and to go as far as possible.

Dare to follow what enlivens and excites you. Don't allow yourself to settle into that rut mentioned earlier. Continually ask yourself, "What do I long to do? Who do I long to be?" Keep questioning what you can do today to move toward that passion. The more you are in a position of activity, the more opportunities will begin to appear. You must be ready for them when they do.

The only way for you to go as far as you possibly can is to be awake and alert and always expecting the best to come to you in the most unexpected ways.

See Yourself as a Winner; as Already Successful

Research from many renowned psychologists shows that most people miss 68% or more of the available opportunities thats are right under their noses.

Why?

It's mainly because they have not programmed their brain to be on the lookout for fresh new opportunities. It's because we're trapped in a pattern of routine, thoughtless habits, and overinflated to-do lists. We are so programmed that we've shut down awareness. We are in a rut of discontent and a self-imposed comfort zone, and while this comfort zone may feel familiar, it is seldom *comfortable*. In fact, it often feels stifling. Because of this trapped pattern, we miss important things that are going on all around us.

This foggy perspective about life prevents us from envisioning all the unlimited possibilities for our lives. But when you see yourself as the CEO of your company, you will also see yourself as a winner. You will see yourself as already being successful in whatever endeavor that you have chosen. In order to *see* yourself as a successful person, you must incorporate the ability to use *techniques of visualization*.

Visualization is a rather amazing tool that requires practice to learn. In the beginning, your dreams and goals may seem rather lofty (and to the natural mind, almost unattainable). This is why it will be crucial that you learn to *see* yourself in the place where you desire to be.

As you learn to visualize your success, it will ignite a sense of excitement and fresh energy within you. That fresh energy will serve to compel you to carry out the daily and weekly tasks needed to achieve your goals.

Once you develop the habit of creative visualization, it will serve you in many areas of your life. In fact, it can help you to achieve most anything that you want in life.

Let's take a close look at what happens when you use your visualization strategy.

As you visualize an event or a goal, in effect it calls your brain to focus on all things connected to that goal. Can you see how counterproductive it is to visualize calamity? Or disaster? Or failure? Or defeat? Have you often wondered why some of your worst fears come to pass? This is because visualization is a principle that works no matter how it's used. Now you want to learn to use it to your benefit.

It's a proven scientific fact that our basic existence is energy and vibration. Each person, you included, is in constant vibration. Our senses are made up of a combination of those vibrations—and how they respond to the vibrations of others around us. This means, the energy you give off will come back to you.

Can you see then that visualization is simply based on sending signals to the universe? Your thoughts are manifested in events and things. It is not magic, no more than the principle of gravity is magic. Do you marvel that when you drop something it falls to the floor? You would be more surprised if it floated away from you. Likewise, you should be surprised if your ability to envision success *failed* to work for you.

Listening to a successful person, you will hear them talk about their nature, or their personality, or their talents and abilities, but at the root of it all, it comes down to the thoughts of success that they hold in their mind. Successful people visualize achieving their goals. Unsuccessful people visualize their excuses and the many reason why *can't* achieve their goals.

It was Henry Ford who said, "*Whether you think you can, or you think you can't—you're right.*" Consciously or unconsciously you will become the very person you think you are. The more you see yourself as a success the closer you are to achieving the aspirations for your life.

The Value of Correct Habits

The practice of visualization mentioned in the last section is a *habit*. Whether the visualization is negative or positive, it is a habit. Habits are little-understood by most people, and often thought to be harmless. Most people are at the mercy of their own destructive habits; their unproductive habits rule their lives. The truth is, it is attention to habits that can mean the difference between failure and success. As we all know, there are good habits and there are bad habits. The habit of cleanliness and personal hygiene is a good habit. The habit of overeating and making poor food choices is definitely a bad habit that can lead to illness and possibly premature death.

Some people have a habit of making mindless purchases while watching a shopping channel on television. Some are addicted to endless computer games. Still others have a habit of continually criticizing other people around them and so, now that habit has taken over. Even when that person wants to be kind, it's difficult to do so. The habit has become entrenched.

What's happening here? Let's look at habits from a clinical or a scientific approach.

Repeated behavior creates *pathways*—for want of a better term—in your brain. The longer the behavior exists, the more defined that brain pathway becomes. Picture a fenced yard where the family dog has worn a deep, well-established path along the fence. This *dog-run* is packed down soil and no grass will grow there. The owners may wish to have a flawless lawn, but no wishing will make it so as long as the dog runs on it every day and as long as that deep furrow exists.

This can be compared to your wishing that you could change your habit patterns. It will take more than just will-power or wishing. For instance, you may want to change your habit of negative, failure-based thought patterns. Instead, you want to develop positive thought patterns that envision success:

thought patterns that see opportunities, solve existing problems, and overcome any obstacles that are in the way. The best and most effective way to do that is to begin to fill your mind with constructive, confidence-building, and illuminating information.

In other words, you will replace those negative thought patterns with positive thought patterns. This can be done through reading, listening to podcasts, attending online webinars, and attending live seminars. As has been stated, we are living in the information age, and good information is at our disposals in many various forms. How sad that so much is available and so few people are willing to take advantage of it. (More about life-long learning in the next section.)

You can never change what you fail to acknowledge. When it comes to the harmful habit patterns in your life, it will require facing hard facts and being totally honest with yourself. Take the time to identify the habits that are pulling you down, and then seek ways to replace them with productive habits. This breaks those pathways that have become ingrained.

Let's say that you have embarked on a good exercise program, but your ingrained habit is to crash on the couch the moment you arrive home from work. *It's just for a few minutes,* you tell yourself. *I'll just catch up on the news and watch the weather report.* The next thing you know, you've wasted an hour.

Your plan to interrupt that old pathway is to unplug the television, and place your running shoes right by the front door. It is a creative solution that will trick your mind into creating new mind pathways. Make your own list of solutions that can work in your particular situation.

Your goal in this step-by-step wealth action guidebook is to create and maintain a lifestyle that will be conducive and favourable for success opportunities to flourish. This can never happen as long as you continue to allow unproductive habits to rule your daily life.

Take the time to make a list of the habits that you know are not beneficial to achieving your goals. I mentioned earlier about having a critical nature. That someone who is constantly critical and demeaning of others will have few friends. If this is a problem in your life, have the courage to face the problem and write it down. As you write out your list, soon you will have ideas coming to your mind of methods by which you can replace the destructive habit.

For that critical person, an idea would be to set a goal to compliment at least three people each every day. This new behaviour pattern will eventually take over and replace the old. Soon you will be looking for the good in people rather than always finding fault. Such strategies can change your life for the better.

Education As Distinguished From Learning

Yet another way to change your life and change your wealth status is to understand the difference between *getting* an education and *being involved* in the process of learning. Those who fail to understand these two very different processes are destined to live far short of their intended potential.

The first difference between the two is that education comes from outside of self. You sit in a classroom and listen to a teacher; you read textbooks. In this process, knowledge, values, skills and attitudes are imparted to you. Learning, on the other hand, is the process of *adopting* knowledge, values and skills for yourself. Learning evolves through your inner self.

Education is usually for a set period of time. For instance, a person may graduate from high school or college and consider her education process as being complete. Learning, in one way or another, however, goes on for a lifetime. Education revolves around a particular set of standards; learning has no set standards. Education is considered *formal*; learning is more informal.

It is a sad indictment of today's society that many people finish their education process and see *learning* as complete and over. It's also a sad indictment that many young people emerge from our formal educational systems never having learned *how to learn*. Nor did they learn to *enjoy learning*. This is especially disturbing in light of the fact that technology and the world market are changing at the speed of light, and those who are not prepared to continually learn new skills will be left behind—as will all their dreams and aspirations for continued success.

This quote from Peter Drucker clarifies the point: *"The only skill that will be important in the 21st century is the skill of learning new skills. Everything else will become obsolete over time."*

Take inventory of your own life. What new skills are you learning today? This week? This month? What efforts have you made recently to learn about a new subject? Or a new strategy in which to accomplish your goals?

Take this inventory a step further—or a step deeper. What is your basic attitude toward learning? Is it something you enjoy? Or is it something you dread? Have past experiences with the education process left you with negative reactions about learning? If so, then it's even more important that you come to grips with the difference between learning and a formal education.

A distaste towards learning new things may be due to some fear that stems from past experiences. This often happens when an individual suffers from adverse experiences in the school system. This includes the student who was unable to get the needed grades, who might have been set back a grade level or two, or who was made fun of due to an inability to perform well in the classroom. Any of these experiences may very well translate over to a distaste for any type of learning. A deep-seated fear prevents them from stepping out to learn new skills. The old memories and old behaviour patterns say, *I can't do this.*

This is why it's important to understand that your ongoing learning is quite different than studying rote facts about history or math in your middle-school classroom. This is where the visualization that we talked about earlier will be a needed skill in your new life. You can begin to visualize yourself not only learning new skills, but becoming highly adept at using them.

Make a list of skills you will need to accomplish your objectives, and to achieve the goals you have set out for yourself. These will be skills in which you may now be rusty, or skills you have never learned. For instance, later in the book we will discuss how to invest your money in the stock market. It may sound like a scary proposition to review a company report—and not only to review it but to understand it. It will be especially true if mathematics and numbers were never your strong suit. This is a skill that can be learned.

Even the skill of public speaking, which many people admit is fearful to them, can be learned. Not only are there workshops and books relating to speech anxiety, but there are also coaches who can walk a person through the process of overcoming this fear.

Whatever it is that you need to learn, if it is part of the longings of your heart, you can attain the needed skills. You can even overcome your reluctance to learning. Embrace the realization that lifelong learning can be the foundation upon which you will build your new wealth status. It's all a part of investing in yourself.

Mental Health

Several things that have been discussed in this section on *Self Mastery* have had to do with your mind and your thought-life, or, in other words, your *mental health*. This is true when we discussed knowing yourself, knowing what you want (and what you don't want), how to develop good habits, visualization, and lifelong learning. All of these areas have to do with your mental health, or the inner attitude of self. It has been said that "success is 80% attitude and 20% skill."

Even though that is true, it's amazing how many people spend an entire lifetime looking outside of self to attain success. They believe that if they get the best education or land the right job, if they get the best promotions or own the right business, or even if they are connected with the right people, they are on their way to success.

It doesn't take long to look at the people around you and see that that's a myth. There are highly educated people who are inept at people skills or at problem-solving skills. There are people in high-paying positions who are unhappy with their lives.

It goes back to what was discussed in Chapter 1 about what success means to you. What is it you truly *want*? And in order to discover that, you must get off the hamster-wheel existence of doing the same old thing day after day. You must take the time to reflect and dig deep inside of yourself to know who you are and what you want.

As was mentioned in the section on lifelong learning, no matter what it is that you need to know, there is a book or a course or a seminar or a webinar on the subject. You can learn what you need to know.

I often tell people that their biggest enemy is themselves. You can become anything you want to become, but first you must get past the enemy of self.

<u>You</u> are the person telling you that you can't do this, or you can't do that. It's that inner voice that says you are too short, too tall, too ugly, too dumb, too different from others, and on and on the list goes. This is why you need to work on *you*. Because, now that you know what it is that you want to do, it's time to start feeding your mind with the information that will take you where you want to go.

Now you are going to be reading, listening, going to seminars, networking, and socializing with people who are going in the direction that you want to go. This is the quickest way to do it. Everything you do should be around the subject in which you are interested, because that's what you want to do. That's what you have decided you want to do with your life.

Feed Your Mind

It's time to start *feeding your mind* with information. If you are in your car commuting to work every day, what should you be listening to? Some people just listen to music all of the time. But why? Is the music taking you where you want to be?

Probably not. Instead, you could be in your car listening to teachings that will teach you what you need to know, in order to get where you want to go.

What about people who don't drive? Use your mobile phone with an MP3 player. Or simply purchase a cheap MP3 player. You can upload content and listen to it when you are on the train, or while you're out jogging or working out. Feed your mind with something that's making you better tomorrow than you are today.

What about reading? If you are sitting on a train every day, why not read a book that will teach you the information that you need to know. It has been said that if you read one book a week on one subject, in about a year you'll become an expert on that particular subject. This means that anyone can become an expert if they choose to do so.

This is all about working on *you*. This is about making you the very best that you can possibly be. The only person who is going to do that is you. Feed your mind with good information just the same as you would feed your body with good food. It's sad that people are so much more apt to feed their bodies than to feed their minds. In fact, they seem to prefer feeding their minds with garbage which will take them nowhere.

This usually refers to those who have no idea what they want or where they are going in life. Because they have no direction or purpose, they are content to feed themselves with anything that comes along. If that once described you and your life, it describes you no longer. You are now extremely conscious of exactly what you put in your mind, and you are careful about what you feed your mind.

Grow a Thinking Mind

Thinking is hard work, which is why you don't see a lot of people doing it.

—Sue Grafton

Yet another aspect of mental health is the ability to be a critical thinker. A common trait found among successful people is the fact that they are *thinkers*.

And not just average thinkers but very good thinkers! In today's world, thinking is almost a lost art.

Many of us sit down to ponder from time to time and actually feel we have successfully engaged in fruitful thinking. Sometimes when meditating on the various aspects of the world or wherever our thoughts may lead us, when interrupted we might be heard to say, "Sorry I was just thinking."

If asked what it was you were thinking about, however, you may spend another hour or so trying to figure out exactly what it was that you were thinking about. The truth is, just *having thoughts* does not constitute thinking. We all have thoughts. We all have opinions and beliefs—usually lots of them. But just because there's mental activity going on in our minds doesn't mean we're *thinking*. William James once wrote, *"A great many people think they are thinking when they are merely rearranging their prejudices."*

When Albert Schweitzer was asked what was wrong with the world, he replied: *"They don't think enough."*

Edison agreed when he said, "*Our greatest need is to teach people how to think—not what, but HOW.*" He further added: *"There is no expedient to which a man will go to avoid the real labour of thinking."*

Bob Proctor in his book, *You Were Born Rich*, writes, "*Thinking is the highest function of which a human being is capable.*"

Clearly put, all of these men were of a mind that thinking is hard work, and demands more of us than most of us realize. No doubt thinking *is* hard work. Maybe that's why so few people do it.

> "What is the hardest task in the world? To think."
> —Ralph Waldo Emerson

So what is the *real thinking* that we are referring to? Another term for this is *critical thinking*. You can find many different explanations and definitions of critical thinking, but one that is simple and easy to understand is as follows:

> *Critical thinking is disciplined thinking that is clear, rational, open-minded, and informed by evidence.*
>
> —Dictionary.com

When Abraham Lincoln came into his first term as President of the United States in 1861, he stepped into a cauldron of anger and unrest. Half of his nation had declared war on the other half. Who was right? Who was wrong? And how was he to handle all of the mundane details as well as the major decisions that came as a result of the raging war?

This called for critical thinking on a daily basis. In hindsight, it's easy to second guess every move Lincoln should have made. Did he make a few mistakes along the way? Of course. He was human. His biggest mistake early on was placing implicit trust in his generals, many of whom were incompetent. However, overall—on average—the majority of decisions that Lincoln made were crucial to saving the nation.

Hundreds of other leaders can be cited as examples of how clear and critical thinking saved lives, saved nations, and changed history. On a smaller scale, business leaders can be cited as having saved entire companies by their ability to use clear and critical thinking.

For us personally, what's so frustrating is the fact that there are so many unthinking people around us. And to our detriment, it's these very people that we surround ourselves with. What's worse is the fact that most *people's thoughts are usually someone else's opinions*. To a great degree, we live in an *unthinking* generation. We do things not because they make sense, but more so because they make sense to someone else who somehow convinced us of their sensibility. Without so much as a question, we embrace other people's thoughts with no consideration for the risks attached to the act of *following without thinking*.

Hitler is arguably one of the most crazed human beings who ever lived in history. He annihilated millions of innocent Jews with the help of his followers, most of whom were unthinking people who massacred of an entire generation. You may argue that the man was insane and a dictator, and that it was impossible to dare go against his beliefs. But isn't it more insane to not think? To actually sit by and watch as millions lose their lives for no reason at all? No reason except for the warped belief that they are of a lesser group?

So stop to consider—are your thoughts your own? Or do you think only what others persuade you to think? Are your thoughts clear, critical, and with purpose? When you find yourself surrounded by people who are not driven by conscious thought, you would be well advised to extricate yourself from such association, or your progression will become stunted and your decline, swift.

But why is it that we don't think anymore?

I believe one reason is that we're so busy *doing* that we don't have time to conceive, deliberate and consider. It's so easy in our age of technology to be consumed by mindless activities: watching television, checking email, reading texts, following social media.

Add to that the fact that we are constantly inundated with information. It comes at us so fast that we have little time to reflect on much, if any, of it. We see incidents on TV, read it in glossy magazines, see it on the Internet, or listen to our leaders who tell us what to think when what we clearly need to do is learn how to think ourselves. But for the most part we're lazy, and we just want the painless way out of any dilemma, despite the fact that life is neither easy nor simple.

I love to read, but I'm convinced that the greatest value in reading is not the information, but rather what we think about while we read. (That's why *what* we choose to read is so important.) Thinking is the highest faculty of the human mind—the *key to all progress*. As has been stated, thinking is hard work!

Keep in mind that the objective of education is not only to fill our minds with information, but to also stimulate our mind to think and ponder and reason. The value of our studies is increased a thousand-fold if we are able, from time to time, to contemplate upon what we've read, and think about what it means and how and why it might apply to us. Even better is when we, at the very least, surround ourselves with knowledgeable persons. There is nothing so bad as being a part of a conversation that you know nothing about, where everyone is equally misinformed.

The most precious resource we have is our time. And time is more worthwhile if a sizeable chunk of it is spent on thinking.

Remember: clarity is power. And clarity only comes from thinking.

In the next chapter we will move from the internal to the external by discussing the importance of outward impressions.

Chapter 5

Outward Impression

Physical Health

The physical body in which you live is irreplaceable, and yet we see people abusing their bodies as though they could trade it in on next year's new model. While it's important to set a course to become a successful person in life, it is all for naught if you risk your health to obtain that dream. If a business owner works relentlessly to build up a business and then is able to sell it and have a good retirement but is too ill to enjoy retirement, of what use was any of it?

Physical health is an area that I continue to work on in my life. I have never had a weight problem; on the contrary, I've always been rather skinny. But it's easy to forget that even thin people can have health problems, too.

Your body is the supporting system of your mind, and if you are constantly ill or feeling tired and fatigued, you will not be operating at your optimum level. It's ironic, but there are owners of million-dollar race horses who feed their horses better than most humans feed their bodies. Additionally, those horses probably get more exercise!

I'm sure you've noticed, but poor health can be extremely expensive. Doctors, hospitals, and prescriptions cost a great deal of money. This is why making good health a priority is a wise financial investment.

There was a time in history when people ate because they were hungry, and their food was full of needed nutrients. In today's society, however, people eat because they just *feel* like eating—not always because they're hungry. And they eat foods that have little or no nutritional value. They are called "empty calories." Junk food, per se, will add no fuel to the engine that is called your body. Not only will it not add fuel, it will instead cause a great deal of harm.

The amount of available information that is available today on wellness and nutrition leaves everyone without any excuse. Scientific evidence overwhelmingly proves that many of today's most common diseases such as diabetes, heart problems, stomach disorders and so on, can be prevented and cured by a healthy diet. It is such a simple remedy, and yet it seems many would rather take a pill than take responsibility for their own health.

Don't let that apply to you. You are on a journey to take yourself to a higher level—to a more enriching and fulfilling life. For this reason, you are determined to become more disciplined about your own health. Carefully study our own eating habits. You may think you eat *pretty well,* but upon closer study will find that you have a great deal of room for improvement.

We talked in the last chapter about mind and thought habits. The truth is, poor eating habits begin in the mind. This is where eating disorders such as binging originate. The good news is that changing eating habits is not difficult. It takes making the decision, and then applying the needed discipline.

If you have ever been around someone who has lost their health, you know only too well that no one can put a price on a healthy body. Since that is true, and we know it to be true, why do we put just *any type of food* into our bodies? Sugar-laden soft drinks, heavily caffeinated coffee, salty snack foods, and grease-filled fried foods put more of a strain on the digestive system (and all vital organs) than one could ever imagine.

It's time to ask yourself, why do you eat? Do you eat to take good care of your body? Or do you eat just to be doing something—and anything goes? Only you can answer those questions. But be very honest. If you are serious about taking your life to the next level, you cannot ignore this vital area.

Stress and Anxiety

It's amazing how few people connect the dots between nutrition and the problem of high anxiety.

But the truth is that food items such as caffeine, sugar, and alcohol work to elevate stress levels. The irony of this is that most people drink a cup of coffee to calm their nerves when exactly the opposite happens—once the caffeine high is passed. Caffeine can actually work to trigger panic attacks because it accelerates the heart rate.

I am not an expert in health and nutrition but my research tells me that there are many whole foods that work to calm nerves and lower anxiety levels. Let's just look at one example—whole grains (for those who can tolerate gluten). Whole grain foods can have a powerful effect on anxiety, and contain nutrients that have been stripped out of modern day diets.

- Whole grains are rich in magnesium, and magnesium deficiency may lead to anxiety.

- Whole grains contain tryptophan, which becomes serotonin—a calming neurotransmitter.

> Whole grains create healthy energy while reducing hunger—both important for anxiety.

And while you are examining your diet and making healthy improvements, be certain that you are drinking as much fresh water daily as possible. 6-8 glasses is not too much, and is a critical support to your health and wellbeing. Growing up, I lived in a village where the water was so dirty it looked gray. It is a luxury we have, to be surrounded by excellent filtered or spring water, and one to take advantage of. If you are feeling thirsty, it is already too late!! You need to drink water throughout your day, with extra amounts after exercise, just to stay properly hydrated, and supportive of the body's natural healthy systems.

Take your own initiative to learn as much as you can about how the foods you eat affect the way you think and feel. The more aware you become, the more pro-active you will be in your own wellness quest.

Other techniques for the battle against extreme stress can include: deep breathing exercises; getting a good night sleep; and making sure that your schedule contains a good mix of work, play, physical activity, and relaxation.

The importance of exercise cannot be overemphasized. When you are anxious and under duress, your body fills with adrenaline. The trick is to transfer that adrenaline towards aerobic activity. Here are a few ways that exercise works to control anxiety symptoms:

> ➤ Exercise burns away stress hormones that create anxiety symptoms.
> ➤ Exercise tires your muscles, reducing excess energy and tension.
> ➤ Exercise releases endorphins which improve overall mood.
> ➤ Exercise forces healthier breathing.
> ➤ Exercise is a healthy distraction.

Make sure you are involved in some kind of aerobic activity at least three times a week, even if it's only a brisk walk through the neighbourhood.

It's a fallacy to think that stress is just a part of life and has to be *endured*. Truth is, stress can be detrimental to your health in a number of different ways. Stress that is not restricted can contribute to health problems such as high blood pressure, heart disease, obesity and diabetes.

Don't let stress and anxiety cost you your future. Take steps today to bring it under control.

Presentation: Look Successful; Act Successful

Young people today seem to have lost the ability (or the desire) to create a good appearance. Many who have been unsuccessful in finding gainful employment don't realize how important it is to look, act, and feel the part (role) they want to *play*. It involves a degree of arrogance to declare,

"This is how I am, this is who I am. I shouldn't be judged on how I look. That's not what's important."

You can think these thoughts all day long, but you will never achieve the success that you are seeking. The fact is, it's only human nature for someone to take a look at you and come to a quick conclusion. That conclusion might be one of the following:

> *If this person doesn't care how he looks, perhaps he won't care about the job he is applying for.*

> *If this job opening doesn't deserve being well dressed, perhaps this job candidate doesn't deserve the job.*

> *If our customers were to see this person as a representative of our company, we're done for.*

> *If this young woman doesn't understand the importance of a well-groomed appearance, what else doesn't she know or understand?*

> *If this candidate doesn't have enough self-respect to present a good appearance, he may not have the confidence needed to carry out this job position.*

We live in a world where we are first judged by our appearances and second by our brains. While this may not seem fair, let's face it: life isn't fair. And I am not talking about looks, as looks have to do with what you were born with. You can do nothing about your looks. Appearance, on the other hand, has to do with how you carry yourself and how you dress, and <u>this</u> is something you can improve for your benefit.

Whatever career path you choose, your appearance should be in tune with the group that you want to belong to or associate with. If you're a business man (and you're neither Richard Branson nor Bill Gates), then dress like one.

A study was done by two economists, Daniel Hamermesh and Jeff Biddle. They used survey data to examine the impact that one's appearance has on a person's income. In each survey, the interviewer asking the questions also rated the respondents' physical appearance. Respondents were classified into one of the following groups: below average, average and above average.

Results of the survey came up with the following two conclusions:

a) A person with below-average looks tended to earn 9% less per hour, and an above-average person tended to earn 5% more per hour than an average-looking person.

b) For the median male working full-time, their respective penalty and premium ranged from $1,400 to $2,600 annually. While the corresponding penalty and premium for the median female worker ranged from $1,100 to $2,000 annually.

So we can safely conclude that beauty is not just in the eye of the beholder, but in the eye of your bank account as well!

There's an old saying, *"You never get a second chance to make a first impression."* And the first impression is the last impression. It is as true today as it ever was in the past. Presenting a professional appearance gives off the aura not only of confidence and success, but also portrays a clear-thinking, high-reaching individual.

It would seem a simple matter of common sense that attire that is great for the beach or for yard work, dance clubs, workout sessions and sports events is not acceptable for the workplace—or for a job interview. But business owners and others in hiring positions can testify that such common sense is rare these days. Even if a job candidate has the aptitude and skills for a certain position, their sloppy appearance can cause them to be turned away.

It cannot be overemphasized how crucial it is to look the part of who you want to become. I have touched on the outward appearance—good grooming and a choice of a professional wardrobe. But it's also important to *behave* like the person you want to become.

When you are dreaming of the person you want to become, the time to start acting like that person is today. Stand tall, stand and sit up straight (no more slouching), hold your head up, look people in the eye, give a firm handshake, and exude the confidence of that successful person you know you can be. (And soon *will* be.) In the last chapter, we talked about the power of visualization. Here is an area where you can put that concept to work. See yourself as that successful person, and then walk it out each and every day.

Think Like a Leader; Act Like a Leader; Be a Leader

It is very rare that those who are highly successful in a certain field are good at being subordinate. They are usually inventors and early adopters. They are usually out in front of the pack. If they ever have to follow, they do so wisely, aware that at any time a chance will materialize that provides them with that opportunity to finally break free. Even average successful people are seldom found hanging around in the back of the crowd.

An intimate look at the great successful men of our time will show you that these great men and women were always busy forging a path for others to follow. They go their own way. They sometimes take risks that others may deem foolish, but in the process, they achieve success.

Being a leader means breaking away from the crowd; moving away from where *it's all happening*. And I say this objectively. Many of us prefer the crowd, perhaps because we like to hide and it's much more comfortable and safe in there than out in the real world. In a crowd, there's really no need to make big decisions. Someone is already there doing all the thinking for you.

You must know, though, that if everyone is following then there must be a problem somewhere because, where the masses tend to follow, more often than not they are following mediocrity. True achievers are not mediocre. They are leaders making their own calls and facing the consequences of their actions.

But for some of us, we cannot see that we are destined for something more. We are so wound up in our own issues that we cannot take responsibility for anything.

A young teenager named Erik was visually challenged. He was told from early on that he would one day be totally blind. In spite of that, Erik attended college and became a classroom teacher. Erik was not what was considered a *normal* blind person. He didn't do what other blind people do. He was always out in front of the pack.

In his teen years, his father took him and his brothers on hiking adventures around the world. Erik began to nurture the idea of scaling some of the larger, more formidable peaks in the world. Today, Erik Weihenmayer has successfully scaled the tallest mountains on all seven continents—including Mt. Everest. This would certainly be a big enough accomplishment for any person—let alone a sightless person—but is not all for Erik. He is also an author, speaker, acrobatic skydiver, long-distance biker, marathon runner, skier, ice climber, and rock climber.

Erik serves as an instructor and encourager for every sight-challenged individual in the world. His leadership role, built on courage, strong character and integrity, is an amazement to all.

Self-Mastery

Some may say that leaders are leaders by nature—they are born that way. By defining leadership in this manner, we tend to ignore other factors that define leadership outside of our innate being, such as our environment. We also need to be aware that the skills of leadership can be *learned*.

Isn't this the reason why we have mentors and seminars, to teach us its basic principles? In my view, some leaders can also be nurtured and developed just like any new habit can be integrated successfully into one's lifestyle. Anyone can become a leader: it's up you. If you're not a leader already, you can choose to be one. And you can do it today.

Chapter 6

Reach Out to Others

Kindness Can Go Viral

In the previous chapters we concentrated on self-mastery, how to understand who you are, what you want, and where you're going. In your quest for a higher level of success and a more fulfilling life, you must at the same time reach out a helping hand to others around you. It's true that you cannot help others if you have not helped yourself first. That is why the first part of the book is designed to turn your attention toward making you the very best you can be. At this point, then, it's time to reach out and help others.

It is often thought—however erroneously—that in order to get to the *top,* or to get where you are going in life, you have to grab and take and step on others to get there. The fact is, a balanced life is a life in which giving back is part of the equation. Acts of kindness nearly always make the giver feel better about herself. Plus, those same acts of kindness make the recipient want to pass it on and likewise be kind to others. Acts of charity and kindness can become contagious and spread virally.

Kindness as a Sign of Weakness?

Still another erroneous assumption is that acts of kindness can be perceived as a sign of weakness in a leader. The leader should be tough and hardnosed in order to run a tight ship. Here again, this fails to take into account that giving, helping, and extending acts of kindness can do nothing but cause an individual to grow in both an emotional dimension as well as a spiritual one. To the confident leader whose identity is built on a strong foundation, it will not matter if being kind and gentle is perceived as a sign of weakness. That leader knows better, and will be the winner in the long run.

Studies have shown that in sales, for instance, the individual who from is willing the outset to go the extra mile both for their colleagues and their customers, achieved higher sales ranking than their counterparts. This was due to the fact that they earned the trust of their customers and the support of their coworkers. So it stands to reason that giving back can be a beneficial lifestyle—especially when the giving comes from the heart, and is not performed simply as a way to chalk up *extra points*.

Consumed by All the Takers

Another complaint often heard on this subject is that, if you try to be nice to everyone and anyone, you will find your time consumed by all of the *takers* in life. Isn't this just another way for a person to be exploited by those who really don't care?

This is partially true. But it can happen only when the true givers are careless enough to put the interests of others totally ahead of their own. They unwisely sacrifice their time and energy, which then renders them unable to help much of anyone. Then answer is to set clear boundaries and maintain a good balance. This means to balance the concern for others with maintaining a handle on their own interests.

It is absolutely impossible to help everyone all of the time. The giver who comes out ahead is the one who is careful to give in ways that benefit others, but, at the same time, are not incredibly costly to them.

Giving back to others and giving back to one's community are ways to become connected with other people. It gives a sense of being less self-centered, and more aware of the needs of others.

When it comes down to it, any business—no matter what industry it represents—exists to add value to the lives of its customers and clients. The business person who loses sight of that fact will soon be out of business. So in effect the idea of giving, and giving back, should be an extension of what is already taking place in the business. It's really impossible to be a complete success in life and still be egocentric and selfish.

Volunteer Your Time

A very important way to reach out to other is to volunteer. If you have well-defined reasons to do anything, be it success or success-related, it is important to understand that the reason why you would want to volunteer your time and effort is to learn more and enhance your education.

It has been my experience that to volunteer is to succeed. I have always been one for volunteering. Whenever there was something to be done, I volunteered my time to do it. This was my strategy to get ahead where others had failed. By volunteering, I created numerous opportunities for myself to meet people who further built me up as a person. This may not have been the path I wanted to follow, but in truth I had limited options. I had an even stronger aspiration to become independent fast, and one day go back to my home country and make a difference to my people.

Something that I must add, though, is that when you are out to learn, be sure to seek out someone who is ten times better or more successful than yourself in whatever field interests you. You will learn more. Reason being, such people are usually more willing to reveal to you their secrets of success honestly and candidly because they are not threatened by you. Seeking advice from someone who is equally trying to get ahead may not always work as well. They will see your potential, and because they do not want to be left behind, will rarely be of much help to your ambitions.

Several years ago, I attended a business seminar in London where I happened to meet a man whom I had for years wanted to meet due to his raved-about intelligence and influence in high places, primarily in business circles. I was elated to actually have an opportunity to share a speaking stage with him. I was even more elated when I got the opportunity to have an exclusive one-on-one with him.

For some reason, he had been impressed by my speech and overall achievements (minor as they still were to me), and wanted to perhaps understand how I managed to do so much with so little. You can imagine my disappointment however when, as soon as we got chatting, his initial and subsequent questions thereafter for the entirety of our brief conversation were focused solely on my *educational training*: which good schools or universities I had been to and the like.

I could see in his eyes the awe he had held for me slowly dissipate as he realised I had hardly any formal training. For some reason, he couldn't quite handle how it had happened that I'd managed to make such outstanding progress in business outside of it. He was clearly a strong believer in degrees and educational distinctions of some form or other; our entire conversation, which I opted to cut short, was a questioning one because the man just could not stop attempting to discover if there was some secret school somewhere in my past life that I had refused to divulge.

This meeting left me wondering if truly formal education is the only route to success, and from then on I made it my mission to study people, like myself, could not boast of having had that privilege.

Monetary Giving

Giving and reaching out can also take the form of giving monetarily to worthy causes. Philanthropy is never out of vogue. Successful people habitually place giving right at the top of their financial responsibilities. They know that the law of sowing and reaping works in every case, even when it may not seem like it, at the moment. It's a universal law that affects the giver and the recipient, both, in a positive manner.

If you take the time to do research, you will find that there is no shortage of worthy non-profit organizations that are doing work in the community and that fit with your interests and passions.

Choose one or two such organizations, and become their most eager supporter and cheerleader. You will feel better about yourself, and the organizations will be ever so grateful. Non-profit groups cannot exist without financial backers who believe in their causes.

◆ *Self-Mastery* ◆

Teach Your Children about Money

Another way to reach out to others is to take the time to teach your own children about money and financial matters. Don't assume that they will simply *catch it* on their own. They may not. It's a sad state of affairs that, in this present culture, a young person can graduate from an institution of higher learning and be drowning in credit card debt because they had no clue how to budget their money. How can this happen? It happens because parents are handing over this responsibility to the school systems and to society as a whole. This is doing no favors to the children.

As the parent in the home, you are the leader who needs to teach your children about earning money, handling money, and making money grow. If they are not taught these basic principles, they may very well fall to the bottom of the heap in this highly competitive world market.

The time and energy you invest in teaching your children will never be wasted. It will give you great pleasure in later years to see them making wise financial decisions when they are out on their own.

Never Too Late

No matter where you are on your journey to build a more successful lifestyle, it is never too late to begin giving—whether the giving is through random acts of kindness, in mentoring a young person, in supporting your charitable interests, or, as has been mentioned, in teaching your own children about giving and other financial matters. If this has been a missing piece in the puzzle of your life, don't hesitate a moment. Rectify that problem today.

Chapter 7

Learn from Others

Learn From the Best

One of the quickest and easiest ways to take a shortcut (so to speak) to success is to find a person, or persons, who are successfully doing what you want to do and learn from them.

At the tender age of fifteen, I left my home country of Uganda and landed in London. I had a plan to get a job in order to sustain myself, then to purchase products to ship back to Uganda where I would sell them all for a profit. I could speak very little English, and this huge metropolis was a source of confusion to me.

To get an edge on what was going on around me, I made it a habit to get my hands on all kinds of reading material which of course tended to be skewed towards business subjects. I knew that I would get nowhere if I simply hung out with young people my age. I had to take a different approach. While my peers were hanging out at parties and drinking, my sole occupation became, first, to devour all kinds of business books and then, second, to read out loud all through the night in my studio apartment in an attempt to perfect my English pronunciation.

I enrolled in business school and took seminars in my spare time. I wanted to learn from the best. I was not too keen on taking year-long courses because in my mind I needed the knowledge in a month or less. I was already running a business, and I knew that I could learn most business aspects in a shorter period of time as long I was learning from those who had done it already.

So, to make up for time, I began listening to audio tapes and CDs, and watching videos that covered all aspects of business ranging from sales, marketing, accounting, financial services, economics, and public speaking to English as foreign language.

I did not doubt my ability to compete with the more educated; and where I couldn't compete, I employed the best people to represent me. It was actually simple. Smart people are always looking for jobs where they can help dumb people like me succeed without having to spend years in colleges.

I was trying to perfect my speech and accent. Since English wasn't a foreign language to me, I was also having a serious problem with its alphabet. On numerous occasions my poor articulation proved to be a public embarrassment, much to the joy of my English friends who were fast making me out to be the African clown who couldn't speak English to save his life. So, to learn more of this strange tongue, I hung around people who had English as their first language.

I remember being in my room once when I heard people knocking on my front door. When I opened it, there were 2 young men the Church of Jesus Christ of the Latter Day Saints (the Mormon Church). Once I realized that English was their first language, I wanted to hang around with them.

We went out 3 nights a week, teaching Bible studies. I used to watch them and listen to every word they said, and then repeat it word for word in my head, practicing how to pronounce each phrase that they used. I remember that, one time, I heard them talking about me, how keen I was. What they didn't realize, however, what that I was really only hanging around them to learn how to speak English. Don't get me know wrong: I *did* enjoy going around and teaching the Bible! But I had other reasons to be there that they never knew about, which was a funny thing for only me to know.

I later opted to become a speaker and a coach— activities that significantly improved my speech and pronunciation.

As a result, I began to attend all kinds of business and English-speaking courses in my free time, some of which included English as a foreign language, English for beginners, business English, you name it.

As luck would have it, by this time I had already selected my calling to engage in business; without this conviction, perhaps I would have instead ended up as an English teacher.

So, when I say that it's important to learn from those who are successfully doing what it is that you want to do, I am not just handing out casual, untested advice. I am speaking from years of experience.

The Importance of Association

With this in mind, it is evident that in the preparation for success, *association* is one of the most powerful factors. So powerful in fact that, if the associations are not of the right kind, failure is inevitable. Just as one diseased sheep may contaminate a flock, so can one evil associate—particularly if he is daring—damage the morals of many. Most everyone can remember the one bad kid at school who had a negative effect on others around him. But few can so readily point to the schoolmate whose example and influence were for good. This is because goodness, though more potent, seldom makes itself as conspicuous as vice.

Why is it that a person who has been confined to prison will come out into freedom and go right back to their former life? It's because that person has spent months and years in the presence of those whose lives are as messed up—or more so—than his own. He has spent all of his time learning their habits, their attitudes, and their ways of thinking. How can it be expected that he will emerge from such a negative situation and be ready to become a law-abiding member of society?

In light of this, to become successful and wealthy, aside from opportunity and the ambition, you will need a teacher or mentor. By identifying the kinds of associations that best suit your success-ambition, a mentor will help you begin to refine the route you should follow. This is usually someone who shares your same success or career path; additionally, it is someone who has the time to be your mentor. There is no point selecting someone who is too busy to give you enough attention.

So, as long as the person you choose as your mentor is someone who has some form of experience performing to a high standard, and who operates within a role similar to the one you're in, plus is truly interested in helping you to acquire the skills and knowledge that you need, then you're in safe hands.

Don't discount the effect of home and family as being part of the mentoring that you have received. It's mainly in the home that the heart is opened, habits are formed, the intellect is awakened, and character molded for good or evil. For example, I was taught early, from a long-standing tradition, that the man was the provider of the home, and should be looked up to at all times.

Despite the fact that I was not yet fully grown, the war that was brought to our part of the world decades before by a ruthless government helped to catapult me into my manhood. It became my responsibility to care for an entire family. Were it not for my upbringing, perhaps I would have abandoned my business aspirations and done what many other boys my age chose to do at the time (many of whom had no other alternative), and that was to join the army. Because of my home and the positive associations I had been exposed to, I chose not to forget what was instilled in me by those whom I looked up to and loved.

For example, my mother used to tell me that she could smell from 100 miles if I had smoked a cigarette. It may sound funny, but I believed her!

She also used to say, *"Treat people with respect and always do your best you can."*

Now it's time to move into a set of questions that will make clear to you how you can choose the leaders that you want to emulate. Perhaps, before now, you never gave this a passing thought. Maybe you never spent quality time not only asking hard questions like the ones below, nor did you take the time to evaluate the company you keep.

Is it time for you to make a few adjustments? This doesn't mean you have to be cruel or unkind to those with whom you have been spending much of your time. But for your own sake and the sake of your

◆ *Self-Mastery* ◆

future growth and success, it may be time to move on. This may not happen overnight, but with determination, over time, you can change your circle of friends.

Once I had someone say that you are the average of the 5 people with whom you spend the most time. That day I decided to really choose my friends carefully.

Answering these questions will help you in your search for a mentor.

Character and Leadership Exercise

➢ Name at least twenty qualities of character that you believe make up a successful person.

➢ Identify three main people, places or situations that have been a major influence (for good and bad) in developing your personal characteristics.

➢ Identify at least three people you know, or you know of, who exhibit an honourable character. These are people whom you admire or wish to associate with.

_____

_____

_____

➢ Do you see a trend in these people and how they associate with others?

➢ What could you begin doing in the next 24 hours that would in some way emulate the individuals you admire?

Find Five People: Three Local and Two International

Using these guidelines, I suggest to those who are dead serious on moving toward the top of their niche market to do the following. It's now time to take positive steps to locate those whom you want emulate. You can find out everything you need to know by learning from others who have gone before you.

Take the time to research the leaders in the area of your main interest or expertise. Your first assignment will be to find three local people who are doing exactly what you want to do, and find out how they are doing it. If you can make personal contact with them, that is great; but if not, you can still learn what they are doing and then do the same thing. If it works for them, it will work for you. Perhaps they have written books on their methodology. If so, get ahold of their books and read them all.

Attempt to make contact by commenting on their blog site, or through their social media sites. Ask questions. If an email address is available, contact them by email and, again, ask questions. Be bold enough to ask if you can meet with them to learn more. If the answer is no, then so be it. But if it's a yes, you will greatly benefit from such a personal connection.

If you do set up a one-on-one meeting, do not waste that person's time. Be prepared with well-thought-out questions. Keep the meeting short and to the point. That is, unless your guest wants to keep talking longer; if that's the case, it's a bonus for you.

Do this with all three of the local entrepreneurs whom you have located. From there, extend your boundaries and locate, online, at least two leaders who have an international influence in your chosen niche. In the same way, connect through social media by making yourself visible—not by being a pest, but by asking intelligent questions. Also, again, if you can connect by email, do so. Let this person know that you have been following them, that you admire the progress they have made, and want to learn more.

With today's technology, it's not difficult to set up a Skype call no matter where on the planet that you, or they, live. If that person is willing to give you the time to chat, by all means take advantage of the opportunity.

The more you *hang out* with such influential people, the more you will learn. And the more you will be able to envision yourself enjoying their same level of success.

Be Open to New Concepts and New Ideas

I feel sorry for closed-minded people who are too timid to step out and learn new things, or who refuse to embrace new ideas.

When I arrived in the UK from the country of Uganda as a fifteen-year-old boy, do you think I had a few adjustments to make? Do you think I had a few new things to learn? The two places were like night and day in differences! This story will illustrate my point.

When I arrived in this new country, I had about 350 pounds in my pocket. I was walking along the street and there in a showroom window was this car—a Nissan. The car had a price sticker on it. That was new to me. In Uganda, you never see the price sticker on a car. This car was selling for 300 pounds. I had enough money. I knew how to drive. But I was only fifteen years old, and I wanted that car. No one was there to tell me yes or no. So I bought it!

In Uganda, when you buy a car, you just drive off and that's that. (well what I thought) I had never heard of insurance, taxes, road certificates, or a driver's license. I had no idea that I needed all of these things.

When I drove up to my friend's house, he said, "Did I just see you driving up in a car?" When I said yes, he began to tell me how, if I were to be caught driving without all the necessary papers, I could be sent back to Uganda.

That frightened me. I now had a car that I could not take back; and if I were deported, they would impound the car. I would lose it altogether. I had to quickly ask questions and gather needed information in order to drive my new car legally. I learned exactly what to do, and took the steps to get it all done. Soon, I was driving legally. But I had to accept these new ideas and ways of doing things. Sometimes, lack of knowledge can be your strength. I didn't know what I could or couldn't do, so I tried everything.

What new things will you need to learn in order to become the successful person that you want to be? What new ideas will you need to embrace? What new concepts have you learned thus far by reading this book? Beware of getting stuck in a certain mindset that hinders your growth. It can make the difference between your staying in that deep rut of *sameness,* and launching out into becoming the person you have always longed to be.

Ask Lots of Questions

In the episode with buying the car, I would have been in big trouble had I not started asking lots of questions. Some people are hesitant to ask questions for fear that someone will think that they are ignorant. They are afraid to admit that they don't know something. In my first few months in the UK, I asked questions continually.

I remember how I got to set up my first company in London. Because of my lack of a good education, I knew that for me to get into the job market, let alone getting a well-paying job, was not going to be an easy task. So my primary option was to create a business of my own.

I did work in a factory for a time, but I used to go home crying with a lot of pains in my back so I had to try for better job. Everywhere I went to apply for a new position, they asked me for a work permit (a document that foreigners need to work in the UK; something I did not have). So the only easy option was to sell things, In that process of looking for things to sell, I came across people who were attending to seminars where you could learn anything. I found out that you didn't need a work permit to set up a business, and that it was <u>much</u>

easier to setup a company than to get a job in England!

I also learned something else there that truly changed my life: ***"for everything that you want to do or become there is a book, workshop, seminar or people that are prepared to teach you."***

Now, in the UK like many other developed nations, they have job centers where the unemployed can seek employment. As a young teenager from Uganda, I was surprised to find out how easy it was to get a basic job, and what was even more amazing was the fact that, once you get employed, you have to work 30 days before getting paid. At the same time, if you do not perform per your employer's expectations, you swiftly and justifiably get fired.

I couldn't believe such civility. Where I came from, you got paid at the end of every working day. I could not at any one time trust that my boss would pay me after thirty days!! (Of course, times have changed since then.)

Anyway, this little discovery provided me with an interesting opportunity. Around that time, I was thinking about how to go about starting up my own business. I had the fortune to meet a few presentable and well-spoken Brits who understood the UK system; one was willing to help me to look around for a viable product to sell.

With his help, I found a telecommunications company that was looking for agents to sell its products to other companies. Now, I knew that the product was good; all I needed was an office plus a team of telemarketers, some sales people to send out into the field, and an office administrator. Easily, I got the telemarketers and sales team from the job center. My friend doubled as the front office manager and administrator; I was in charge of pushing sales. But then we needed an actual office, to give the appearance of professionalism.

We went to the library and found books on the subject of *How to Get Free Rent*, and *Offices with Six Months Free Rent*. We learned that, if you go to new buildings or buildings that are undergoing renovations, they are empty or partially empty. The owners are happy for someone to move in, clean them up and make them look good. If they're working on the building, you can ask to move in early and they will give it to you for a time rent-free.

Once we learned that, we started to look for buildings undergoing renovations, and found one with a "To Let" sign in the front. Upon making an inquiry and providing a postdated check (since the building was going to be ready in two months), we signed an agreement and were allotted space.

How did this happen? Because we were open to new ideas and asked lots of questions. And also because we realized that, no matter what it is you need to know or need to learn, somewhere there's a book or a seminar or an audio on the subject from which you can learn.

In Part II, we will look at ways in which you can begin to build your wealth, as well as create multiple streams of income to ensure a solid financial future for your new life.

~PART II~
BUSINESS MASTERY

Create Multiple Streams of Income

Chapter 8

You are a Business

In Part I, *Self-Mastery,* you discovered what you really want in life. You discovered the direction you want your life to take in order to live out your dreams; in order to live a full and satisfying life. That knowledge alone should be very freeing for you.

In this section of the book we will talk about the second phase of building wealth: *Business Mastery.* It is absolutely vital that you become well-informed and knowledgeable about many aspects of business. It is impossible to become all that you want to be in life and not have a high level of business acumen.

Become Knowledgeable about Business

At the outset of the book we discussed the fact that you are the CEO of your own business. That you, in fact, *are your own business*. This mindset will take you a long way down the road of fulfilling your dreams. I encourage people to take on this mindset even when they are working at a full-time job.

You are the CEO and chairman of your own company, and there is absolutely no reason why you shouldn't take charge of that. You need to believe with full conviction that this is your life and you can control it better than anyone else. You alone know your innermost dreams and aspirations, and it's in your power to go after those dreams. You are not at the mercy of other people or circumstances. You are not a victim; you are a victor.

In close relationship to this concept is the decision you make that you *are going to be wealthy*. This is a conscious decision that you must make. You must become convinced of this fact.

Many people may think to themselves that they *might* become wealthy one day in the future. But this is not what I am referring to, because attaining a significant level of wealth is not something that *just happens*. It comes about when you make a deliberate decision and say, "I *will* be wealthy. I *will* find my wealthy place in this world." You may want to write this out in your journal or your goals book, and keep it ever before your eyes.

Once that decision has been made, it will change how you think and how you behave, and it will affect the decisions you make. Once you make that commitment and you are serious about it, there will be things in your life that must be eliminated. This may be activities or it may be certain relationships. The world is full of distractions, and if your decision wavers because of distractions, you will squander your time and attention, and you will never achieve your own goals. Your time is valuable and you must invest it wisely. Make sure that the activities you engage in are consistently moving you toward your goals.

Learn New Skills

In Chapter 4 it was stated that the person who succeeds in today's marketplace is the person who is continually learning new skills. Now that you know the direction you want your life to take, and now that you have made the serious commitment that you *will be wealthy,* assess what skills will be needed to move you in that direction.

In Chapter 7, I told how I spent endless hours reading books aloud in order to perfect my use of the English language. Additionally, I read a wide variety of business books. I knew with certainty that my passion was in the realm of business. I was fascinated with every aspect of starting, building, and maintaining businesses.

I started my first business when I was only a teenager, and since then I've set up more than thirty businesses. I was young and I would come upon an idea that excited me, and I went with it. I was focused on my drive to become successful.

Ten of the businesses, I sold. Five, I still own. Others just fell by the wayside. I was involved in sectors such as financial services, real estate, real estate development, accountancy, publishing, computer software development, management consultancy, and corporate trading. I also had a travel company. I ventured into oil and gas, and was also involved in commodities.

As can be imagined, in order to become successful in such a wide range of industries, I never ceased learning new skills. Being a willing student is a prerequisite for acquiring wealth.

Understand What Makes a Business

In order to buy and sell businesses as I have done, I had to learn how a business works from the inside out. I had to understand all the aspects the structure, the growth rate, management, how to understand financials, and how to make a profit.

Anyone who starts their own business will need to become familiar with all of these business aspects. Much of this, as was mentioned earlier, can be learned from others who have gone before you; those who have already done what you now want to do. Learn from the best and mimic what they do.

Business Should Give YOU Life— Not Take the Life YOU Have

The business that you start up should not be a prison for you. Yes, you are seeking to come into a wealthy place, and yes, there will be a great deal of work to be done. But you are after a lifestyle, and that lifestyle should not be a 60-hour workweek even though, at the beginning, you will have to put in all the hours required. But understand: this is temporary.

As you are going back over your goals list, remind yourself of why you are on this journey. Remind yourself that you want a balanced life that gives you time to enjoy things. To enjoy time with those you love. To be able to do the activities that you want to do when you want to do them, and where you want to do them.

In order to achieve this end, you would do well to stop periodically and take inventory of your time and efforts. It is not necessary to work yourself into a state of illness just to get a business up and going. In fact, one of your goals should be to have a business going that will essentially run itself. *I dedicate an entire chapter to evaluating your and improving your business in order to give you more income and more time.*

Another way to even out your workload and increase your income is to have multiple streams of income.

Reasons Why Not To Put All Eggs in One Basket

In the most recent economic crash, it was heartbreaking to see long-term employees lose their jobs and retirement pensions simply because it had never occurred to them to diversify and build other streams of income. Old-school thinking taught them that having a good job with a good company that offered good benefits was all the security needed. They found this myth shattered when everything came crashing down. Not only was all of their income coming from one source, but most had only one investment vehicle, as well. This is one of the most basic reasons why you need to consider creating multiple streams of income.

The Example of Richard Branson

When you think of the richest people in the world or the most successful, the name Richard Branson easily comes to mind. How did he become so wealthy and influential? Several reasons. We know he has been a risk-taker, unafraid to try new things. He is hard-working, ambitious, and motivated, somebody who loves people, energetic, shrewd, and wants to make a difference in the world. But there's one other element in his ability to build wealth: all of the different business undertakings in which he participates, or has been involved with, in the past. If you research his businesses, you will find over 400 that are under the umbrella of the Virgin brand.

You may or may not be interested in having that many businesses, but you get the idea of how important this aspect is when it comes to building wealth.

Accelerate the Process

Another aspect of multiple streams of income is that it accelerates the wealth-building process. You will grow your financial base much more quickly when the income is coming in from more than one source.

And then there is the point of security. When you have multiple streams of income, there is no need to panic when business is slow or you lose your biggest client, or you just have a need of extra cash.

The very best part about multiple streams of income is that anyone can create them. You don't have to be a financial wizard, or a business mogul.

With the help of today's amazing technology, you can begin to build your own multiple streams of income.

In the next few chapters we'll take a closer look at exactly how this can be accomplished.

Chapter 9

Making Money with Information Products

The Information Age

We live in the *information age*. People get on the Internet to find information and to learn things. What is it that you know that some other people may not know—or at least, they don't know as much about it as you do? Is it your hobby? Or perhaps it's what you are doing now for an employer, but you're fairly confident that you know enough about the niche to provide information online about it.

What is it that you enjoy doing so much that you would actually do it for free? You have such a passion for it and it's something you would do, even if you never made any money from it? Whatever that subject is, you can be making a lot of money with what you know.

You may have never thought of this before. That means that opportunities are right at your fingertips and you've never taken notice. Marketing with information products is a great way to begin earning a passive income. You can take your knowledge and your passion and capitalize on it by creating information products and sell them on and off line.

Books & E-Books

The first place to begin in developing information products about your unique niche or expertise that you can sell online is a book. Whether a paperback or e-book or both: this is a powerful, simple, and ideal product that you can tackle right away.

Now, the thought of writing your own book may frighten you at first. You may say, "I'm not a professional writer. I can't do this." But you can.

I believe that anyone can write a book. Half the battle is to just begin and then, slowly and surely, do a little bit every day. For example, if you write just one page a day for 3 months, you can complete an entire 100-page book! You could start, for example, by listing the ten most frequently asked questions about your expertise, and then ten more things that you really think people should know. You'll easily be able to write 5 pages on each of the 20 ideas, then add some information about how you became an expert and what qualifies you to share or teach this topic, and you have a beautiful and interesting book!

Or think about a book that teaches a skill or technique that you know well in 10 easy chapters. If you're not excited about facing a piece of paper, give yourself those 10-20 topics and then speak out loud to a voice recorder. Transcribe everything you say—or hire someone to type it up for you. *Rewriting* your book based on all of that material is much easier than starting with a blank page.

Another alternative is to team up with someone who can write for you. In this scenario, you provide the information to a ghostwriter, whether through a series of phone interviews or notes and outlines that you have done, and that author will write the book for you. Where do you find such a person? Check out sites such as Elance.com and Guru.com. Both of them feature different types of professional writers to whom you can outsource work such as ghostwriting, proofreading and editing, and then formatting your book so that it is professionally presentable for publishing on various platforms.

There are tremendous, simple opportunities for self-publishing books these days, and with a little research, you too can see your products available at Amazon.com and on your own website; you can also print them as attractive paperbacks to sell at lectures or seminars, buy them at a very low "author's price" of a few dollars, and sell them for $10 or $20. You provide the information, and the ghostwriter writes the book for you.

There are *so many benefits* of your writing a book. First, a book establishes you as an expert in your field. Second, it becomes your first marketing tool, communicating in a professional manner your skills and expertise, while attracting new clients for your services, seminars, or other products. Third, you will make money from every copy that you sell.

To publish your eBook, Kindle Direct Publishing (http://kdp.amazon.com) is website where you create an account and set up your manuscript, which you can do for free or with the assistance of another freelance editor/formatter; you will price your book between 99-cents and $9.99 and receive 30-70% royalty on every book sold. CreateSpace.com is the Amazon-owned self-publication site most easily accessed for paperback printing. It offers a step-by-step process to ensure that your book looks great, then sells it both there and on Amazon in any quantities that you or your customers order. Here, you can price your book from $9-$99, depending upon your expertise, value and popularity. You also receive the lion's share of royalties, or can print low-cost royalty-free copies and self them at point-of-purchase locations.

Audio Books

If you were to record yourself reading your book, you could sell the audio version. Many busy people in today's world enjoy listening to audio books while they are driving, commuting, taking a walk, or working out. If they are interested in your subject matter, they may prefer to listen to the material rather than read it. Audio books are a market niche that is thriving these days, and if you don't like your own voice, you can hire someone to read it for you.

You will need to create digital files that are downloadable from iTunes and Amazon. Both have sites to assist authors and other sellers to set up accounts under their label and brand. But remember: you can also create an MP3 file or series of files that you make available for download from your own website (which we discuss later). You can set up a PayPal account and email the link to verified buyers. It takes some energy and attention to handle your own fulfillment of these orders, at first. But it is well worth it, and can be automated or outsourced once you grow in size and populatrity.

Special Report

Once your book is completed and online ready to sell, take a chapter or two out of it and create a special report. A special report can be used as a freebie—a giveaway product that is used to draw visitors to your site. Or it can be used as material for blog posts which then builds content created by you around your expertise, and establishes you as a published, knowledgeable person in this niche.

Remember: people buy from people they know and trust. So you should take this and other opportunities like blogs, eNewsletters, and guest-postings to create good content that you can give away for free to people in order to help them get to know you.

There are many websites and social media interest groups (through LinkedIn, Huffington Post, Facebook, alumni groups, guilds and associations, etc.) that are very welcoming to posts, guest columns, or regular blogs and essays. Each one that you publish attracts new eyes to your products, new attention to your services, and additional credibility to your brand and expertise.

Collect anything that you post elsewhere in a special section at your own website, with attributions/credits, so that you can watch your body of self-generated content grow. When other customers or experts comment on some of your content, add that to your site, as well. It further helps to expand your appearance of influence, community, and credibility.

PowerPoint Presentation

This information from your book can also easily be adapted into a professional a PowerPoint presentation. Condense your thesis and findings into slides with key concepts and images. Your presentation can be used in a workshop or a seminar, as accompaniment to your talk and lecture.

It can also be animated, which turns it into a video presentation that can be featured on your website as a dynamic graphic, and on YouTube, where it is easy to establish your own free "channel."

In order to record your PowerPoint presentation, you may use programs like Camtasia Studio (Windows) or Screen Flow (Mac). These sorts of software are ideal ways to record any presentation or other information that is displayed on your desktop.

In expanding or extrapolating your material from a book or eBook, consider enhancing your PowerPoint with additional graphics in order to make it more visually appealing. This is much more interesting than just reading words on slides!

Webinars

A webinar is simply an online live seminar where the audience can interact with an expert or teacher by asking questions in real-time through an instant messaging tool. As the presenter, you can share PowerPoint presentations, videos, web pages, or other multimedia content with your audience, too. And the amazing thing is that the audience can be from anyplace around the globe.

A webinar is a perfect way to introduce new materials or new products. While no webinar should be designed only for selling, after your new or important information has been presented and your audience's questions answered, you have an ideal opportunity to introduce your products so that customers can go deeper, learn more, or stay in touch with you.

This is also a great way to increase your exposure and your online following. Webinars are the fastest-growing trend in online marketing, and the best way to reach new and ongoing customers all over the world. Consider participating in a few to see how they work and what you like about them. You'll find it easy to duplicate and make your own.

One-Day Workshops

The information that you are compiling and organizing can be set up into a one-day live workshop. Many communities have meeting room available in hotels and other civic center locations. Advertise your event among your friends and colleagues, via email, notices in local calendars or papers, and on Facebook plus by printing flyers or messages in areas frequented by your clientele.

On the day of the event, hire a professional videographer to record your event on HD. Even if there are only a few people in attendance, your presentation will appear professional, and be able to be repurposed as a DVD series or even transcribed into your next book!

Information marketing is a potential goldmine for you and your company. It has many aspects and products, each one of which should be well-produced, consistent with your message, and promoted in order to increase both your prominence and your income.

These one-day or weekend seminars can be priced anywhere from $99 to $5000, depending upon your experience, the value you offer your customers, and your growing popularity.

Audio, DVDs and Home-Study Courses

Once you have a video of the one-day workshop, you can now create a DVD Home Study course. There are companies that will create your labels, replicate the DVDs, package them and distribute them for you. Some home-study courses sell for hundreds of dollars. Can you see how information products can quickly escalate your income?

Home Study Courses are very popular and they are premier products. The average Home Study course is selling for $997 per sale, while they can range from $99 to $4,997 depending on your experience, value and popularity. They may include 5-10 educational DVDs plus another 5-10 interviews with other experts. They may be a set of DVDs with a workbook that you print at CreateSpace or a downloadable PDF. There are many ways to package your talks and teachings into a modular set of lessons that can be viewed, absorbed, and appreciated by clients in their home.

Consulting, Coaching, Group-Mentoring

It is very possible to take the knowledge that you have in your selected subject and set up a consulting business. You can teach others what you know. This can be done online in a webinar, or can be done live through one-on-one consultations by phone, in person (if geographically possible), or by Skype.

There are many people who learn better in a private conversation where they can ask questions as they come up, rather than listening to a webinar or watching a presentation. This is where the private consulting comes into the picture. And of course the more personalized the attention, the higher fees you can charge.

In some instances, this is a short-term program; in others, you can design an entire coaching plan that takes private clients or a small group of mentees through the steps necessary to learn some aspect of your expertise.

This is but one more step in your product line that packages and promotes the information that you uniquely know. They key is to develop any or all of these, in sequence, with an eye to maximizing your material and your message.

At first it may be advantageous to work with a professional coach who can help you develop this entire line of information products around your expertise, and ensure that your message is consistent and valuable. You also want to partner with production and formatting professionals (like DVD producers, videographers, writers and editors) so that your materials and packaging look amazing, and you have support in any technical arena that is not your specialty or skill set.

Licensing

As you develop a brand that becomes well-known, it will be possible for you to sell licensing rights to other business entrepreneurs. They can become licensed distributors of your products, which is a great way to leverage your efforts. Your books and DVDs are offered through their websites, at their events, and to their stakeholders and communities.

The exciting thing is that the world is open to your products, and people are looking for partners all over the world! It does require some research and fulfillment to develop these relationships and to attract licensing requests. You also need to do a contract with any partners who handle your products to ensure that your message and brand remain high quality, and that revenues are divided equitably.

Affiliates/Joint Ventures

Yet another way to leverage your efforts is to create products that can be sold by affiliate marketers. (There is more about affiliates in the next chapter.) People will sign up to market and sell your products. You can reach more customers and add a nice (passive!) income stream by recruiting affiliates to sell your product for you. They get a percentage and you get a percentage. But they are doing all the work for you. It's an incredible way in which to earn passive income.

Affiliate programs can be created for physical products (such as crafts, jewellery, clothing, or food items) or digital products (like e-books, audio files or video tutorials). No matter what it is, you'll sell a lot more and earn a lot more when you have hundreds of other online marketers selling for you.

Professional Speaker

Becoming a professional speaker will place you on the speaking circuits where you can earn sizeable fees. In addition, speaking engagements will further help to establish you as an expert in your field. This is an area where, as a young teenager from Uganda, no one would have dreamed I could have achieved such a position. But to date I have given professional presentations in over twenty different countries, and have shared the stage with some of the most well-known speakers in the world. Additionally, I have been featured on hundreds of radio and television shows.

You may not believe that you have the wherewithal to accomplish this feat, but if you want it badly enough, you too can do it. You can learn; you can train; you can practice. As has been stated earlier, find someone who is doing it, and learn from them. I assure you, it is possible. Just believe in yourself and get out there and do it.

Sponsorships

There are certain products and situations that may attract the sponsorship of corporations or non-profit organizations. They may align with their message. They may be ideal member benefits to be given to their community, based on your unique message or presentation. Or they may speak to a need of corporate management to train, educate, or inspire their employees.

There are many unique avenues to research for how to offer, purpose, and even fund your products and presentations through corporate HR or responsibility departments and initiatives. I am particularly adept and creative at brainstorming these sorts of strategies, and helping you to develop the plans and relationships where you can approach and profit from sponsorships. Feel free to email me if you would like more information about this: info@actionwealthsystem.com, and put "Action Wealth Sponsorships" as your Subject Line.

Unlimited Possibilities

This list could go on and on, but I think that you are getting the picture! There are endless ways for you to create, and earn from, information products. The added advantage is that the more that you produce, the more professional you will appear to be. The more professional you appear to be, the more people will trust you, and your sales will begin to grow exponentially.

I firmly believe that you, too, can make a million dollars by teaching others what you know and make only be taking for granted, at this point! You need to do the strategic thinking that identifies the depth and breadth of your expertise, and then maps out a path for developing, producing, and then marketing information products that speak to your audience, and that meet the need of your customers.

Again: this may be best done with a coach who targets your specific niche and who provides skill in creating a pathway to profits from your knowledge and unique message. But there is no doubt that these products generate substantial income, and are the very best way to maximize on your expertise, in the long run.

Chapter 10

Making Money Online

A Level Playing Field

You may not be aware of this fact, but the Internet is making a lot of people very rich. The amazing thing about this is that they are people from all walks of life and from all parts of the world. They are of no certain age, they are of no certain level of education. The Internet has created a level playing field for the average person to come aboard, get cracking, and earn extra income.

I've added the chart below to give you an idea of the enormous growth population throughout the world. This will help you to see that this is the future of business and business endeavors. Some will look at this and just shake their head, thinking, "It's so big, I'll get swallowed up and be lost in the crowd."

However, there are others who look at this and say, "This is so big, how can I miss?"

The latter is the truth. The world of Internet opportunities is so large and so vast that there is room for everyone. Even you.

One of the great benefits of earning money on the Internet is that you no longer need to be in an office or in a brick-and-mortar store to have a business and earn an income. You can work from home, or from your vacation spot, or from any point on the globe. All you need is an Internet connection and a computer, and you're good to go. This creates a whole new realm of opportunity.

In this chapter, we'll look at just a few of the ways in which you can get set up a variety of businesses and begin earning cash flow rather quickly.

WORLD INTERNET USAGE AND POPULATION STATISTICS
June 30, 2012

World Regions	Population (2012 Est.)	Internet Users Dec. 31, 2000	Internet Users Latest Data	Penetration (% Population)	Growth 2000-2012	Users % of Table
Africa	1,073,380,925	4,514,400	167,335,676	15.6 %	3,606.7 %	7.0 %
Asia	3,922,066,987	114,304,000	1,076,681,059	27.5 %	841.9 %	44.8 %
Europe	820,918,446	105,096,093	518,512,109	63.2 %	393.4 %	21.5 %
Middle East	223,608,203	3,284,800	90,000,455	40.2 %	2,639.9 %	3.7 %
North America	348,280,154	108,096,800	273,785,413	78.6 %	153.3 %	11.4 %
Latin America / Caribbean	593,688,638	18,068,919	254,915,745	42.9 %	1,310.8 %	10.6 %
Oceania / Australia	35,903,569	7,620,480	24,287,919	67.6 %	218.7 %	1.0 %
WORLD TOTAL	7,017,846,922	360,985,492	2,405,518,376	34.3 %	566.4 %	100.0 %

Credit: www.internetworldstats.com

How Much Money Do You Want to Make?

Your first step will be to decide how much money you want to make from your online businesses. Be sure to <u>write this down</u> in your goals notebook so it will be constantly in front of you. Be sure it's a realistic goal—something that is doable—or you will find yourself becoming discouraged and maybe even quitting before you really get started.

Whatever this desired amount is, be prepared to invest at least 10%-25% of your target income into your endeavors. While you will find that many online opportunities are low-cost and some are free, still you will want to put forth a concerted effort in making this work for you. And that means investing in advertising and various programs that will help get things going.

You only make money when a product or service is provided. In the previous chapter you learned about creating your own information products; however, there are also ways to earn money online without having a product of your own. (More about that later.)

Building Relationships

Making money with online businesses is all about building relationships. This is one of the great benefits of online marketing: social media sites such as Facebook, Twitter, Instagram, Pinterest, and LinkedIn make it possible for you to connect with people. They can get to know you and find out what you're all about. You may have heard the saying that people only buy from people they know, like, and trust. It's true. And by networking on the Internet, you can become known, liked, and trusted. It's definitely a win-win situation.

Earning money via the Internet should not be considered a get-rich-quick scheme, but it is definitely a shortcut to getting rich quick. While there are scores of ways that you can earn money online, we will look at just four of the more well-known methods:

1. Market your own product

2. Affiliate Marketing

3. CPA (Cost Per Action)

4. Media Buys

Market your Own Product

You already know how strongly I believe that it is important to create your own products for sale. Developing a line of information products was discussed in the previous chapter. But perhaps your product can be another off-shoot of your unique expertise, or in addition to the books and instructional materials you create for your brand.

If you're a chef, for example, it could be a line of sauces or condiments. If you're a home and lifestyle expert, maybe it is some practical kitchen tool, or line of bedding. If fashion is your specialty, maybe you have a personal line of jewelry or accessories.

Brainstorming about your specific niche and helping you to create your own products to sell online is one of my top specialties. If you want any help in this area, I am more than happy to help you.

Just send me an email at:

info@actionwealthsystem.com

Affiliate Marketing

What is affiliate marketing? This is where you get paid a commission when a sale is made from a lead that you have generated. The commissions can range from 10%-75%, depending on the product.

The opportunity to sell affiliate products online has been a boon to thousands of people who have discovered that the Internet as a viable income earner. Those who choose the affiliate route have the advantage of marketing an existing product, which means that most of the work is already done. The product has already been created, as has the accompanying advertising and promotional materials like logos, packaging, and marketing language. The work left to the affiliate is to reach out to customers and bring them to that product.

The first challenge is to find a product or group of products that you would like to market and sell online. Where do you find such products? Here are a few of the most popular and well-known affiliate programs:

- ClickBank (www.clickbank.com)
- Commission Junction (www.cj.com)
- LinkShare (www.linkshare.com)
- Affiliate Window (www.affiliatewindow.com)
- Amazon (www.amazon.com)
- Google (www.google.com/adsense/)
- LinkConnector (www.linkconnector.com)

Each of these (and there are many more out there) offer hundreds of products to choose from. Many beginners start out by marketing the most high-ranking top sellers. While this might seem the best way to go, you will also find that the most competition for customers with other affiliate marketers who might be more experienced than you are. A better plan is to find products that are in a niche that interests you. If you are working with products that you use and enjoy, you might find that you are more likely to get excited about promoting them to your networks.

No matter what the product is, the creator of that product has already designed highly professional marketing materials such as landing pages, logos, and banners; some even offer you samples of email sales letters. All of these tools are at your disposal. All you have to do is get the word out there. With each sale that you make, you will receive a percentage of the sale.

How to Get Started

Your first step will be to register an affiliate account with one of the companies listed above. The second step will be to choose a product to market. Don't make this more difficult than it is. True, there are hundreds and thousands to choose from, but don't spend an inordinate amount of time making your choice. Just jump in and get started. You can refine as you proceed. The more that you get involved with the experience, the more you will learn.

Here are a few examples of silos from which you will have an opportunity to choose products:

- Arts & Entertainment

- Betting
- Biz / Investing
- E-biz & E-marketing
- Employment
- Fiction
- Games
- Green
- Health
- Education
- Home & Garden
- Mobile
- Parent & Family
- Politics
- Reference
- Self-Help
- Software
- Spiritual / Alternative
- Sports and Travel

As you can see there's a lot of variety. That's why it crucial that you don't get bogged down in decision-making. It will rob you of your time, and you will never get started.

You Will Need a Domain Name

After you are registered as an affiliate and you know the niche in which you will be working, your next step is to purchase a domain name that will refer to the niche of your product. There are a number of sites where you can find a domain name. Here are a few:

- Register.com
- Wix.com
- GoDaddy
- EasySpace
- CheapDomain
- 1and1

Choose a domain that is easy to recognize, and conveys what you want it to convey. Don't use tricky spelling, and avoid characters, underlines and dashes.

Blog/Website

I always advise those who are beginning in affiliate marketing to use WordPress as the simplest program out there to set up your blog and your website. It's very easy to use, and they provide many professional templates. (You don't have to design your own site.) WordPress works great for search engine optimization (SEO) as well, which will help keep you on page one of the search engines.

In recent months, Wix.com has also become a favorite site for new website builders. It also has many many templates for all sorts of styles and personal businesses, reasonable hosting deals, a simple modular to adding content to your site, and a lot of help. They can also register your domain name and guide you through the process.

Hosting Provider

You will want to choose the hosted version of WordPress or Wix, because it offers so many more options to make your site professional.

If you don't select that option (maybe you have a teenager who can build your template and website gratis!), in order to host your site, you will need a host provider such as HostGator. Also, the site where you purchased your domain name may also offer hosting. Check and see. Compare prices and services. Don't hesitate to call these companies and ask questions. Most have wonderful customer service.

Remember, you are in learning mode here, so don't feel bad because you don't know every answer. Step out of your comfort zone, ask or do research, and find the answers that you need as the questions arise.

Banner

Once you have your site set up, have a professional create a banner for you. You can find such services for a small fee at sites such as *Fiverr.com* and Elance.com.

Create a Killer Bonus

Carefully look over the product that you have chosen. Perhaps it's an ebook on organic gardening. Many people these days want to eat healthy, and also want to save on grocery bills. This particular ebook has shown to be a popular product and sells well. What else can you add to it?

Find what's missing, and then fill that gap. Perhaps you can make a video review of the product. Or you can interview a professional in the field and use the interview as an audio extra—a bonus.

When you create your landing page for your product, tell visitors not to buy the product until they see your bonus. As you add more and more value to the package that you are creating, you will stand out from the crowd. Your business will grow.

Opt-In Form

How will you collect contact information from those who visit your site? It's done by setting up an account with an auto-responder program such as

Aweber and GetResponse. Once you have set up your account, you can create an opt-in form which can be imbedded into your website.

The opt-in form allows each visitor to fill out their contact information and interests. That information goes directly to your auto-responder account, and now you have a new contact. Feel free to provide a gift or bonus to anyone who completes the form, like a special report or recipe or discount coupon on your product. This is how you build your following.

PopUp Domination

If you want to have a greater chance of grabbing the attention of your visitors, use a pop-up. PopUp Domination is one program that is effective and well designed. The pop-up comes onto the page and immediately demands the visitor's attention. He must either fill it out, or click to make it disappear. Either way, it demands a response.

There are many tools such as this that you will learn about in this new business. It all has to do with marketing effectively.

Joint Venture

All over the Internet, there are other people wanting to make a splash in the affiliate marketing world just like you do. Some are your competition; some could become your partners.

Let's go back to the subject of organic gardening. The same audience interested in creating a backyard garden might also be interested in building their own solar-power unit.

Perhaps you could find someone who has a successful blog and website pertaining to DIY solar power, including guides and instructions. This could be a great match. You could place her ads on your site, and in exchange she could place your ads on her site. Again, this is the time to step out of your comfort zone and start to ask questions.

If you call or message or email and make the approach, and the answer is no, move on. That's not the only player out there. If you keep trying, however, you are sure to find someone who would be thrilled to work with you. It's a definite win-win set up where you both will profit. Once you have a partner or alliance, you have a list and that person has a list. Now, your efforts are doubled because you have been featured in front of her audience, and she has been featured in front of yours.

In your search for a possible joint venture, look for the top people who have a huge following. The bigger, the better. Why waste your time with the small operators when you can catch hold and ride of the momentum of the big players?

Start Internetworking

By using some of the social media sites such as Facebook, Twitter, Instagram, Pinterest, and LinkedIn, you can start to network with other like-minded people on the Internet. The marketing techniques that you have at your fingertips used to take business owners many months, and sometimes years, to attain and exploit to their professional advantage. Enjoy this moment in social media marketing! Spend a block of time every day working on your networking skills, and build your online exposure.

Start Making Commission Checks

As you continue to move through these steps and gain the attention of more and more visitors, they will begin to buy from you; your commission checks will come to you with great regularity. This is passive income that will come to you no matter what you are doing, and no matter where you are.

CPA (Cost Per Action)

What are CPA offers? CPA stands for "Cost per Action." It is an advertising model which consists of leads, registrations, free trials, sales, and downloads.

Difference Between CPA and Affiliate Marketing

Are CPA offers better than affiliate marketing? Let's look at a few of the differences.

With affiliate marketing, your income depends solely on your generating a sale. If you drive traffic to a landing page or the product page, but no one purchases anything, you get nothing. However, with CPA marketing, you can send traffic to a landing page with the option that may require only an email address from that traffic—not a full purchase—for you to get paid. In other words, if the visitor is interested in the offer and she puts in her contact information in order to receive more information from the vendor, you will be paid for that, as well.

Networks to Get Started

If this sounds like a winner to you, here are a few networks with which you can get started.

- Neverblue
- Maxbounty
- CPAPark
- AzoogleAds

- Copeac
- Clickbooth
- And many more

Types of CPA Opportunities

Here are a few of the different types of offers that you can get involved in:

- Zip/Post Code Submits—you will get paid from $1-$3.00 per lead.
- Email Submits—you will get paid from $0.85-$2.50.
- Long Form—this involves name, address, email, DOB, telephone number—mainly for car quotes or payday loans; payouts are around $15.00-$34.00.
- Short Forms—this involves DOB, marital status, ethnicity—mainly for dating offers. Payouts are $2.50-$9.00.

➢ Sales—you will get paid a percentage of a product's total price, or a commission off of the total price, usually ranging from 9%-70%.

➢ Free Trails/Sales—you will get paid a certain commission for having the user/customer sign up of a "Free Trail Offer," anywhere from $22-$33.

➢ Downloads—this involves the user downloading a "toolbar," a computer game, or any other type of software to their computer, and once the toolbar, software or game is installed, then you will get paid. Payouts are anywhere from .30-$2.00 a lead.

➢ Pin Submits—this involves the user entering in their cell phone information, and a pin code is set to their phone. Once they type the pin code in on the next page, they can access wallpapers, animation, and lots of other sorts of "infotainment" services for a mobile phone. Payouts are usually $9.00-$12.00 a lead.

As you can see these types of programs can become quite lucrative over time. Again, this is a great way to begin to build up your cash flow and create yet another income stream.

Media Buys

Media Buys refers to your buying banner space on websites or blogs that have high traffic. You pay by the CPM, or the cost-per-thousand impressions (1000 views to your banner). This can be paid monthly or weekly, and the cost will range from $0.50-$20.00.

Here is an example. Let's say you bought banner ads for $2.00 CPM. Out of those 1000 views, let's say you get 200 clicks. If you divide the 200 clicks by $2.00, that means it cost you $.01per click.

Now, what banner will you want to use? Remember, when we talked about CPA offers, I mentioned that those companies provide professional marketing tools—one of which are cool banners. This will be the banner that you use for your CPM campaign. When you promote free offers, it helps you to make the most of your CPA offers. The key is to buy traffic cheaper than you are selling it for.

Summary

Here is a summary of what you have just learned about making money online:

- Register an affiliate account
- Choose a product to market
- Get a domain name (use your product as a key word)
- Find a hosting provider
- Install WordPress and create your website/blog
- Create a killer banner for your website
- Create a killer bonus to be different

- Add on an opt-in form in order to build a list

- Set up a joint venture with another marketer

- Promoting your product

- Help you get accepted with CPA networks

- Create three to five media buys to meet your budget

- **Send me an email** (Subject: *Ready To Get Started*) **to:** info@myactionwealth.com

Now that you know how to begin making money online, in the next chapter you will learn more about setting up a turnkey business that will work on autopilot.

Chapter 11

Making Money with Business Systems

I mentioned earlier that my passion since a very young age is in business, and that has led me to read a great many books on the subject from many different points of view. One very effective idea that I learned, and that I want to share with you as part of my Action Wealth teaching, is that most everything in life can be seen as or organized into an orderly system.

This is important to you for two reasons. First, there are ways to make each of your businesses more systematic, no matter what your product or service, and in this way, make more money by spending less time and managing fewer problems. Second, there are ways to invest your money in businesses that have already done this; they are called *turn-key businesses,* and they can generate additional income for you without the stress and time of founding and managing a start-up.

Systems All Around Us

This may not be something that you have thought about, but your life already includes many sorts of systems and sub-systems. For example, you have your own personal system for what you do when you wake up in the morning. You have another set of patterns or habits for what you do to learn about what's going on in the world around you, whether it is reading a daily newspaper, checking in on *Huffington Post* while you drink your coffee, or tuning in to a cable news show at night. You also already have a way of earning a living that is your income-generation system.

Systems are all around us, and you can use that fact to your advantage as you improve or develop your business. Most people discover that when they design and follow a consistent system for business management or wealth generation, they get the results that they desire. When they follow a well-defined system, they are able to clearly measure those results, as well, and pinpoint areas of improvement. And that's what this book is all about: setting goals and realizing results.

What I discovered in my studies about systems and how they can help you is this: when you or a business is not on a system, you are very likely to spend a great deal of your time running around "putting out fires" instead of figuring out what is actually causing your problem. As my teacher says, "orderliness and attention to detail are the roots of peace ... (and) ... disorder always leads to desperation."

Most all of the problems that arise in the businesses we create are related to a breakdown in one of your systems. So I believe that part of your job as you undertake building optimum wealth is to design systems that deliver the results that you dream of, both at work and in life.

Systems are designed to get certain results. If you're constantly frustrated with something in your business, perhaps you have the wrong systems in place! Or maybe you may just need to change a few steps in a system, and the intended results will come.

Find the Time Bandits

Many people who start and run small businesses are overwhelmed by their work on a daily basis. They start a company or a restaurant or a project because they love it, and it gets to be so consuming that they no longer even enjoy it after a few years.

Usually the problem is that they have become the hardest working employee and the Ms. Fix-it who is constantly putting out fires instead of managing their business. The solution is to develop systems that let the business be operated by your employees or software; this will lower your stress while leaving you more time to develop the business and energy to increase your profits.

You will find that this idea resonates with the ideas of prioritization in Stephen Covey's best-selling book, *Seven Habits of Highly Effective People*. What my teacher Sam Carpenter, author of *Work the System: The Simple Mechanics of Making More and Working Less,* says is "...we are all spiritual beings existing in a mechanical world." We can use this fact to our advantage throughout our daily lives.

There are three steps to developing business systems that will make your business work for you.

First is figuring out your **Strategic Objective**: what it is that you want to achieve. This might be the most important part of this exercise, because it will become your lighthouse, showing you your path and the direction to achieving your goals.

Second, you identify your **General Operating Principles.** These are your basic guidelines for all of the decisions that you make. At this stage, you need to fully document all of the operations that are involved with your project, program, or business. Just the act of doing that will force you to understand that you *have* processes, which is the best way to start fixing them.

Third, and maybe most time-consuming, is to specify your **Working Procedures.** Here, you need to figure out each of the individual systems and processes that make up your business. Write them down, step by step. Systems big and small all have choke points where things may stop or get bottled up; they have feedback mechanisms where you can tell if things are working right (whether from customers, sales reports, delivery on goods and services); and they have points of dramatic improvement.

Figure out which of your processes recur and repeat. It is within this step that you will begin to see what you can begin to improve and how.

Try to imagine your business as an assembly line where things are actually assembled together into a certain process, one at a time. Each *process* then leads to another, in a *series*, and eventually that series repeats as a *cycle*. Remember that goal or *strategic objective* that you identified in step one? As your repeat your cycles again and again, you will reach your destination, and achieve your goal.

To keep growing and improving, you may need to look at your whole process again, making little granular changes in order to meet some challenge that is coming ahead. But because you know your business so well, broken down into processes, if you need to put a new product into distribution or scale up your service line to a new platform or country, you will be able to see clearly *where in the process* you need to make that adjustment or improvement.

So you won't be putting out a fire or dealing with a problem by adding something haphazardly!

Your goal is to systematize each part of your business, and, where possible, assign it to an employee or software program so that it is replicated in the perfect way each time.

The best way to accomplish this task is to take a "slightly elevated and detached" view of the world. Look around you and see how much of everything we do and see is controlled by systems. Then see your own business in the same way.

Work Less, Accomplish More

Carpenter writes about his specific experience at a company that he once ran. He discovered that by clarifying his systems, he was able to improve his employee management, and drastically reduce the amount of time he had to spend at work. After learning to think about his business in terms of its network of systems and sub-systems, and then by studying how to tweak them, he managed to maximize profits, create client loyalty, and develop autonomous employees, all while shortening his work week. Contrary to conventional thought in the 21st century, working all the time does <u>not</u> increase our wealth or happiness!

The classic example of this is the British experience in World War II, where, after the outbreak of the war, factory workers patriotically volunteered to work long hours. After the brief initial increase in productivity, however, there was a dramatic drop in output. The solution was to mandate a limit in the number of hours in the workweek. The lowered length of the workweek brought productivity back up!

Many business owner/operators go through these steps of systematizing their processes, and then they make a huge transition to being just the owner of their enterprise. They discover that they don't have to do *everything* anymore, in order to keep their businesses running. Instead, they put processes, procedures, and people in place to accomplish their business goals, most of which are just to make really good profits. The ancillary benefit is that you get more time to do other things.

Design your Life/Business System

Creating a business system that will work for you without your even being present is not only possible, but is within the scope of your ability. Even beginners can set up such a business in such a way that it improves your performance, shortens your work week, and decreases your stress from disorganization while increasing your profits.

If you are a manager or business owner, always start by documenting your systems on paper. Think about every aspect of your business, from billing to fulfillment to accounting, and figure out which parts can be more formalized. You'll find all sorts of benefits to doing this, from making fewer mistakes to spending less time on them, overall.

Use this list as a tool for work and change, and be sure, if you have employees or partners or subcontractors, that everyone agrees on them.

When something comes up that isn't working, zero in on which of your systems is causing the trouble, and then correct it, specifically. In my opinion, the best use of your time is to spend it on examining and tweaking systems to perfection. I encourage you think about every aspect of your business, from billing to fulfillment to accounting, and figure out which parts can be more formalized.

A Turnkey Business Uses Systems

You also have the opportunity to invest in a business or franchise in which all of the systems have already been established and tested. Such a business is sometimes called a *turnkey* business.

In a turnkey business, a company's high-level management sits down and plans and executes all of the company's business strategies in a way that makes it very easy for someone like you to buy a franchise or business and only "turn the key" to begin operations. These sorts of enterprises already have successful business models that have been proven over time. What you come in with is investment capital, and you either supply or hire the labor.

Franchises are the typical turnkey business, but you can explore an investment in or partnership with any existing business that is already up and running as an opportunity to work with business systems for increasing wealth simply.

Baskin Robbins ice cream shops are an example of a turnkey business. The menu of offerings has been developed, the stores have been designed, the employees' uniforms were selected, there are marketing materials like logos and ad designs and websites already in place, plus consumers already know this popular brand. In order to open a new Baskin Robbins franchise, you would just need to pay the start-up costs for one store location which usually involves a franchise fee, then the operating costs for just that location including some royalty fees back to the company. The great thing is that these systems work already, and you don't have to worry about the other major aspects of business development.

One of the most true and steady ways to build passive income is to set up a turnkey business, get it up and running, enjoy the profits while you are doing other things, and then, in a few years, sell it for an even greater profit. Your job, as an entrepreneur or manager, is to be certain that the systems are maintained, and you are nearly guaranteed success. That is the beauty of a business like this.

There are many things to research and understand, however, in advance. If you are developing a new business, you also want to follow this process and think through your systems so that they can be replicated in cycles.

With these strategies in place, however, you will have even more opportunities to see your wealth grow swiftly and consistently.

In the next chapter you will learn about the need for you to be involved in real estate as another one of your major streams of income.

Chapter 12

Making Money with Real Estate

If you want to make serious income with minimal risk, maximum rewards, and lots of opportunities for everyone whatever your circumstances, then real estate is unquestionably a smart option. They key is to invest intelligently, of course.

It is my opinion that investing in real estate is the second best investment you can make, after investing in yourself. You can never achieve financial success if you don't use (one of my favorite words of all) "leverage." And while there are various ways to save or acquire money to invest in the stock market and in starting your own business, it is even easier to get money in order to buy a property.

Why is that true? Ask any bank or bank loan officer. The reason why any proper bank will give you money on a piece of property more easily than they will for you to start up a small business, for example, is because of this: *security*.

People like to be safe. And banks are no different.

Unlike the average business start-up of selling cars or other goods, **property** is one of those businesses that, even if you fail miserably and default on your loan repayment, the bank can easily repossess your property and recoup their investment in you by disposing of that piece of property. On the other hand, how would they be able to salvage anything from your failed business? Hence the risk of any bank giving credit on a business start-up is far greater than that on property.

So it is important to understand the value of leverage. I will explain and demonstrate this throughout the chapter.

Investing in property is one of the most basic and safe ways for an individual to obtain immense and rare wealth. Neither a huge fortune nor a high IQ is required to start off. In normal circumstances, all that differentiates the average property investor from a billionaire property investor is their ability to apply common sense in decision-making, their motivation, and a steady belief that it can actually be done.

Like all other investment options available, property investment involves *beginning with the end in mind*. What that means is that you want to develop the habit of outlining a clear and distinct picture of your vision for investing in property, even before you begin.

So back to the question, why should one invest in real estate?

Well, for starters, **property** has a unique and universal appeal; a kind of sexy pull towards it. For most people, owning an investment property or renovating a property for profit is generally accepted as a worthy and understandable goal. Over the years, more and more people have become millionaires and billionaires through property than any other type of business.

Secondly, property is ideal for providing you with a predictable and steady income. Especially if you are into buying income-producing properties, as long as you understand the proper strategies required, you are bound to make a PROFIT; you can make an offer on a property, sell it without even owning it, and still make a profit!

Ever heard of the law of supply and demand? Real estate, particularly residential property, is a commodity that is in high demand. It is a necessity and not a luxury, and in many areas there is a shortage.

Another reason why you should invest in real estate is the fact that there is minimal risk compared to other investment options, and it enjoys a track record unmatched by any other investment. For hundreds of years, the value of property everywhere in the world has been going up. Of course there are always those one-off extreme cases where the reverse happens, but these are usually as the result of a number of other factors including unscrupulous business practices and property scams. (For example, the recent financial crisis in the United States property market, riddled with foreclosure scandals that led to a short-term decline in value of property across that country.) But we can safely assume, as is always the case with a market dip in some sector, that this trend will right itself, and prices of property will continue to go back up again.

Additionally, property is a good investment option simply because you can use it as leveraging tool to grow your capital.

Leverage Is the Key to Success

Real Estate leverage is the use of borrowed money to increase your profits in an investment. **Leverage is doing more with less**. When you purchase a piece of real estate, you make use of leverage <u>when you borrow money towards the purchase price.</u>

Building wealth via real estate requires the use of leverage. Let's assume that you have $100,000 to invest, and you purchase a small income property for $100,000 in cash. Let's assume that income properties have been appreciating at an average of 10% per year. At the end of the first year of operation, your property is worth $110,000. At the end of year two, it is worth $121,000. That's a profit of $21,000.

Now, let's assume that you put your $100,000 (10%) down on a $1,000,000 income property and borrow $900,000 from the bank. If the same property's value happens to go up by 10% a year, at the end of the first year, it is worth $1,100,000. At the end of the second year, it is worth $1,210,000. By using leverage, or borrowed money, to purchase a larger income property, you have increased your profit by $189,000 in just two years. *That* is how you the rich get rich: they understand the power of using (OPM) other people's money.

To get the full advantage of leverage, put the minimum down on a good property that has a strong likelihood of appreciating in value.

Leverage with Owner Finance

Suppose you have bad credit. In this instance, you need to learn about **private mortgages**, whereby a seller of a property can "provide you with the mortgage," and you will pay the seller directly, instead of dealing with the bank.

How would this come about? Let us suppose that the seller is already the full owner of his property, and now prefers to earn a monthly income as opposed to his annual returns on the property. In this case, the seller may consider financing the property for you. And, in 99 out of 100 private mortgages, you never incur a credit check. So there's no longer a "bankruptcy" or "no job" excuse to get you out of owning your very own property. Even better, as you're paying off your private mortgage, your property will continue to appreciate in value so, by the time you are done with your payments, you can sell it at the market price of the time!

Last but not least, in inflationary times property has traditionally been used as an excellent hedge to protect one's savings, and can provide you with a powerful, tax-efficient way to build a substantial pension. Although the steps to building a profitable portfolio are relatively straight forward in theory, in practice there may be frustrations and obstacles along the way. But one key point that any property investor must put to mind is that they should be able to see possibilities where others would only see impossibilities.

We will look at some of these aspects as we go further into the subsequent topics. But for now, let's now turn to **setting your real estate goals**.

We Don't Make Land

You are going to take advantage of the fundamental **law of supply and demand.** Real estate, especially residential property, is a commodity that is in crucial shortage, and for which there is enormous demand. It is a necessity and not a shortage. WE DON'T MANUFACTURE LAND! And we know for a fact that there will be more people on the planet tomorrow than there are today. Actually, someone at this very minute IS making babies.

Even if they wanted to, people can't print up 100,000 new homes as they might print up a stock offering. That's why I agree with my friend Robert Allen, who has been heard to say, "**Don't wait to buy real estate, buy real estate and wait.**"

These are some of the reasons why it is so important that you own your own home, for example, and at least a second property to rent. With this information, how can you EVER go wrong?

Set A Real Estate Goal

In this book, we have discussed at length the 3 key aspects of wealth-creation that involve namely: first, working on yourself, followed by the creation of multiple income streams, and lastly, keeping more of your money through the protection of one's assets. In each area, we have identified the need to set goals, and drawing up a kind of road map to wherever you want to go.

As with other goals that you hope to achieve in your lifetime, if you want to accomplish much in real estate, then the first thing to do is scribble down on paper all of your real estate goals.

(If you have no idea what this means, then I suggest that you follow up by taking one of our *Goal-Setting* courses offered by our Action Wealth System learning programmes). Please visit www.actionwealthsystem.com for more details.

Ok, let's say for example that you are a newbie, and have no capital whatsoever to venture into the real estate market. Is this the end of the road for you? Well possibly, but not necessarily. It's never the ideal starting position for anyone to be in, but it's not an unusual one, either. There is always a solution for every problem.

Conventional wisdom may dictate what you can do with your money in order to be a success at property investing, but who said that it has to be *your* money? Once you've realized this and you suffer this predicament, then your next goal would be to find someone who can help you to buy that property.

A second of investing in real estate involves the "WHATs" and the "HOW MUCHs" of this enterprise.

Start out with **what do you want to buy**: a house? A block building? Or maybe, commercial real estate? It may be unrealistic for you to plan for millions of dollars or pounds but if you are already purchasing high rise apartments and property offshore then this may not be too difficult a thing to do. Still, it requires that you put the numbers down on paper so that you can remain focused on your goals.

What kind of property are you looking into: a starter property? A family property? Or a luxury property? And **how much are you looking to earn** from such an investment? If this is your first investment of this nature, then up to now you may have been living from take-home pay to take-home pay.

Once you figure out the "what" and possibly the "how much," the rest of the Q-and-A session on your goals becomes much easier. Take into consideration that your property goals are your own, and cannot be set by anyone other than you. However, you can arrange them in such a way as to benefit not just yourself but others, as well. It is always easier to be successful when your motivation is "self-sacrificing" rather than "self-serving."

Finally, do not measure your goals in comparison to others. Just because you neighbor lives in a huge "fat" mansion doesn't mean that you necessarily have to desire the same thing, too. You must also reflect on the fact that that there are certain other things that are important to you, and **you, specifically**. That is what makes these *your goals:* they are a personal directive, and will inspire your decisions and actions, as you hold them in mind through fruition.

Create a Strategy

Goals are all about what you WANT.

Strategy is defined as that part of your goals that outlines HOW you achieve them.

Real estate goal-setting also has to do with creating, developing, and planning your very own strategy for acquiring property, be it for resale or to keep. *How will you go about it?* You can consider your strategy as a "minor goal" that will help you achieve your major goal. Your number one strategy is to always remain clear-headed and focused. The moment that you start to scan for properties and see more and more "for sale" signs, I guarantee that your property juices will flow. Stay calm!

What is *your strategy* for finding property in prime locations, or distressed sellers who are willing to sell off their homes straight away? What is your strategy for acquiring great bargains?

These are some of the keys aspects that you MUST consider before purchasing any kind of property. You also need to mull over all the aspects fully.

Other features that you may look at whilst developing your strategy are whether you are *planning to be involved* in the property as a business or as an investment. Also, once you choose an area in which to invest, certain aspects of **location** must be considered: is the property near schools, shopping malls, bus stop, train station, hospitals or offices? Once you have determined this, then you can move on to ascertaining the various types of property which I briefly cited earlier.

Do you want income or capital growth? Are you planning to buy a property to keep or for resale? Do you need to take money out of it soon, or later (e.g. for a pension? Or can you let it slowly accumulate?

Let's take, for example, the strategy of acquiring property at this point for resale. In this instance, you may need to look more closely at the short-term value of that particular property, as well as its environs. Can the said property be renovated, revamped, and possibly resold within a short period of time? Are the existing properties in that area already selling within a reasonable time, or are there just too many idle homes waiting to be taken off the market? This same strategy should be covered when looking at properties to let/rent out. Your concern will always be this: the ability to rent a property in the short term in order to garner long-term rewards.

Something else that should be considered as part of your strategy of buying or selling property is keeping your eyes open in order to **get the timing just right**. Successful property investing depends upon TIMING

Firstly, there is the timing of individual deals and when to do them. Then there is timing within the context of the economic cycle. For example, if you are considering buying at the top of the market, you need to ask yourself where the profit is going to come from. Wouldn't it be easier to buy at the bottom of the market, where you are in a position to pick and choose a bargain, as prices are pushed down because no one else is buying? At the top of the market, prices are being pushed up and everyone is piling in and buying. That is the best place to be *selling* and taking your profit, NOT buying and making losses.

Your strategy here is to buy under market value; that is, locking in equity when buying and thereafter allowing the discount to help you to sell under any market condition.

Read Local News

Another part of your strategy is to get into the habit of reading the newspapers, researching more on property, and visiting property auctions, usually a great source of bargains. If you plan on being a serious investor, **print out business cards** and pass them around in order to let people know what you do.

Also, *make friends with the local authorities*; they are usually the first to know about those distressed properties that you may want to invest in, in the future. This information will also help you to decide how much time you have on a weekly basis to achieve your goal.

Once you have developed your concrete strategies, all that is left to do is to **follow through** on them. This is where **accountability** comes in.

To whom are you accountable to keep you on track of your goals?

I believe that, once you understand and apply these fundamental strategies listed about, you will be well on your way to becoming a successful property investor.

Short-Term vs. Long-term Investment

There are some common investment strategies that you want to know as you begin to invest in real estate. Namely: increase in value, double-digit capitalization, and bargain purchase. I will not go into too much detail on these here, but I do believe that it is important for you to familiarize yourself this basic real estate jargon as you begin to enter this business

When you buy property at its current market value and then, immediately after purchase, you make whatever changes are necessary to increase the value of the property, this is the **increas-in-value**

strategy. When you purchase property for at least 20% below current market value, then you are using the **bargain purchase strategy**. **Double-digit capitalization**, on the other hand, simply means that you buying a building on terms that it has a capitalization rate of 10% or more. (Don't worry too much about getting all this right now.)

Short term versus long-term investment strategies are better known as *holding periods*. In essence, you can choose to be a long-term investor or a short term investor (which is also known as a flipper). As the former term suggests, long-term means that you hold the property for years. Most investors do that. This can become a good strategy or you if you are not looking for quick profit, and if the long-term appreciaton rates look great.

Flipping, on the other hand, means selling the property as soon as possible after you purchase it. I recommend flipping for more experienced investors, because this may be risky business despite returns being very profitable. In these stiutations, you hold property for very short periods of time, and the adrenaline is in the turn-over in the short term. The casual observer will discover this trend in the Dubai property market, for example. At the moment, this is a very hot market and a good place to invest if you're looking for great return on your investment in the short term. (Read my book: *"Why Invest in Dubai Real Estate"* and get more insight into the property market there.)

Long-term investing requires much more effort and commitment to maintain than short-term real estate investment; it also requires you to be more aware of what is going on at the local level in the neighborhood and communities of your properties.

Whichever way you decide to go, planning and focusing on your own strategy is key. And always remember to look for and find the possibilities where everyone else sees impossibilities.

Treat This as a Business

If you want to score big in the property game, then you must be SERIOUS about it. The number 1 rule of business is: "To acquire wealth, you must be in a business of your own." I can't simplify that statement any further. So, set up your property investment business like any other.

The good news is that property investing is an easy business to start.

There is no need for special gloves or office space; in fact, you can get started in days, literally. As we discussed in other parts of this book, give your business an identity. Your business name can be one of your best marketing tools, and should create an impression that will attract prospective customers in the future. Preferably use a name that relates to what you do and communicates the same; then, it will not confuse your prospects. Additionally, like in any other business, you will require business cards, logo, brochures, stationery and any other marketing material that is necessary.

Rome was not built in a day, and neither will your property business grow overnight, but you need not treat it as a hobby unless, of course, it is.

Find a Real Estate Mentor

Everyone needs a mentor. As a property investor, likewise, you too **require a real estate mentor.** If you have never bought a piece of property before, how can you do it without the help of some sound advice? Even if you are an experienced investor, as you go along the way, you will realize that every transaction has a learning curve. There are always new things to deal with and learn from.

That's where your mentor will come in, to take you through certain areas that may require a helping hand. Anyone can be your mentor: it's all up to you.

Usually a mentor is someone who already has some form of experience or background in your specific area of interest. They are someone whom you can trust, and who is independent (has no vested interest) so they can be totally blunt and honest when need be. Their primary aim would be to encourage you, give you feedback, teach you new concepts and tricks of the trade, and provide you with a reality check now and then.

Do Your Homework

There is nothing as foolish as purchasing the first viable property you see. Knowledge is the cornerstone upon which any enterprise should be built. It is all about becoming an expert in your chosen area. Like every endeavor we have discussed throughout this book, you want to have adequate working knowledge of your business when you start it, and continue to learn about it as you go along.

Study the property market, both locally and internationally. Even if you don't plan to buy any property abroad, it does no harm to compare the fundamentals of various foreign markets. The more knowledge you possess about your property venture, the more confidence you will have that it will be a success.

So, read for an hour a day about property law, planning and construction, and anything else that will help. Contact estate agents who sell high-yield properties, and start attending auctions where you can start to practice calculating yields and undertaking financial analyses.

Remember that no knowledge is ever wasted, and you can never know too much. When you dive into a pool for the first time with no swimming experience or floaters, chances are that you will drown. So, forewarned is forearmed. Take your time, according to your ability, to absorb and retain information.

Do not be in too much of a hurry to make money. If you must build wealth, build it as a BY-PRODUCT of your business SUCCESS. If wealth is your ONLY aim in business, you will most likely fail.

Know Your Attitude to Risk

What does this mean? Some of us are naturally risk-averse, while others can't help the adrenaline rush that is evoked by the hint of risk. These reactions are primarily linked to our varying personality types. Be aware of your personality type in terms of your aptitude for risk: it is important when considering how to invest in property.

For a smaller, private, or relatively inexperienced investor, the first hurdle can be extremely overwhelming. This is due in part to the perceived or real scale of property. Even the "cheap" properties are relatively expensive and if, for example, you funded it via a loan, it may come as no surprise that you feel very vulnerable and accountable if things don't go smoothly.

However, no billionaire real estate mogul made her fortune by being a sitting duck. So start to look at risk for what it really is: an opportunity to score BIG.

Develop a Winner's Attitude

By now it should be obvious that anyone can afford to be a property investor. But to become rich in property, you must first begin to think and act rich. If you were to walk up to almost anyone and ask that person if they would like to be successful, it will come as no surprise that 99% of the people you speak to will give a resounding YES! However, very few are willing to pay the price, especially when it comes to property investment, because most people don't see it as something that they can do.

To be a success, you must have **a need to be successful**. Everything else must be secondary. You must develop a winner's attitude, start thinking laterally, and see the opportunity behind such a kind of investment rather than just the building, itself. The value of a property depends on the interest being sold and not on the physical accommodation that it provides. Perception goes a long way. **Attitude is 80% of Success, Aptitude Is Just 20%**

Anyone Can Purchase Property

I encourage you to explore and think more about this, beyond my book. Investing in real estate is such an ideal avenue for wealth creation that I have made it a core part of my Action Wealth System!

Remember: becoming a successful property investor is easier than it appears. Anyone can do it— it's just a case of learning the basics and then taking action. I want to leave you with the following image, which shows how the world population is growing in every continent. The reason? Each of these new citizens of the planet will want and need shelter in their lifetime, many of them sooner rather than later. You want to invest and supply property for sale or rent, to take advantage of this great opportunity.

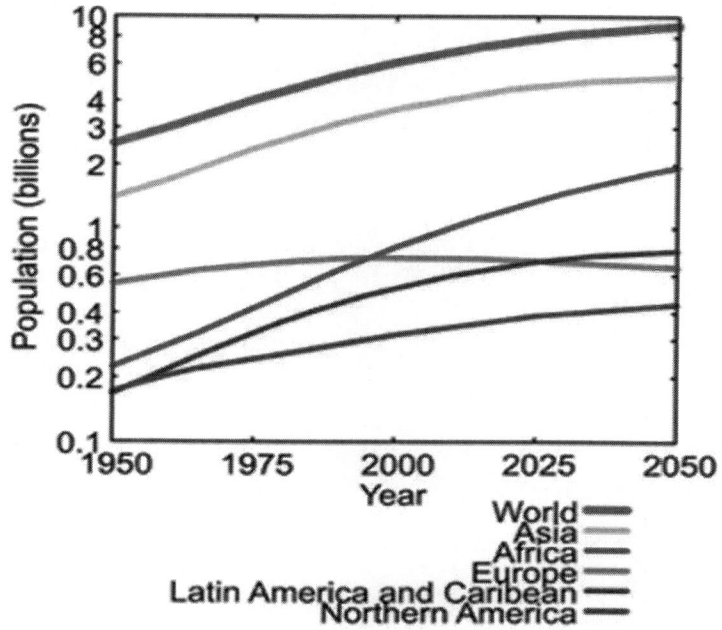

When done correctly, a serious real estate investor can become a property millionaire in three to five years.

The time to start is *now*!

Chapter 13

Growing Wealth as an Investor

Another income-generating opportunity that can help to build your wealth without requiring your constant time and investor is to become <u>an investor.</u> Again, there are many resources available for you to learn about ways to invest in companies and the stock market. I want to offer you some initial keys to investing, and I want to encourage you to take this avenue for wealth creation seriously. It can have tremendous benefits for you!

Investing is for Everyone and Anyone

The stock market is one of the most important sources for companies to raise money. Because of that, it is designed to make you wealthy, when you participate in it over time. The stock market is structured in such a way that it has become a great way to leverage your money, even as a new or individual investor. For a small price, you can purchase your part of an existing company and as they grow, your investment grows.

In years past, investing in the stock market was only for a select few—those who were privy to the information of how it all worked. Everyone had their *stockbroker* who gave them tips and helped them to maneuver through the ins and outs of the market. But that was before the days of the Internet.

In today's world, in this global economy, anyone and everyone can invest in the stock market. Online brokerage services such as ScottTrade, Trade King, and Options Xpress are plentiful throughout the Internet.

Educate Yourself

You can find online courses to teach you the ropes when it comes to investing. You can learn how to choose companies in which to invest, how to read their financial reports, and how to actually make your purchase. Find the most outstanding companies that are strong leaders in their industry: ones that have a good track record and are well-respected and well-known. Learn as much as you can about each company before actually making an investment.

Investing in the stock market is a long-range plan for building your personal wealth. This is an area where you will need to be patient and let your investments grow. This is where compound interest comes into play—your money will begin to grow exponentially.

Take advantage of sites that provide *trade simulators*. These simulators allow you to simulate the act of buying and selling stocks, and are ideal for giving you a feel for the real thing. It's similar to how a rookie airplane pilot learns to fly by using a flight simulator. These sites provide a replica of the real thing, including calculations of potential gains and losses, for your education.

In the days before the Internet this was known as *paper trading*. Instead of working it all out on the computer, the student learned by making all of their investment moves on paper, first. Obviously using a computer is much easier and quicker.

Teach Your Children

In Chapter 6, I made the strong appeal that you to take the time to teach your children about money. It is a travesty to send any children out into the world without their being equipped with ample knowledge about how to function in the financial realm. In fact, I've even written a great book on this subject: ***Financial Literacy for Teens & Their Parents.***

I think that the same applies to sharing knowledge about investing in the stock market.

It's a sad state of affairs when adults believe that information about investing is too complicated for teens to understand, especially when most teenagers today know every detail of a dozen or more computer games. These can be far more complex that the fundamentals of stocks and investing!

Through online research and financial television channels, it has become much easier today to learn the inside workings of any publicly-held company than it has ever been. In the past, in order to learn more about a company, you had to write to or call the company and ask for an investor's packet to be mailed to you. Not so today. Now, you can go to the website of any company, from the oldest Blue Chip corporation to the newest start-up, and learn all about how they run their business. Because they are a *publicly held* entity, all of their information must be *public*. It's all there at your fingertips. It's up to you to take advantage of that information.

You can make it a family game to select companies in which you kids are interested, and let them investigate their financial ins and outs, as a way to learn more about how that company works.

You can teach your children that, if they save their money and purchase one *share* of a stock (let's say they have chosen Apple, for instance), they would then become a part owner in this gigantic corporation. Teach them that, because they have invested in this corporation, they are actually helping Apple to continue in business, because funds from the sale of stock are used by any company to expand, and to do research on future products.

When kids grasp this concept, they get excited and want to be a part of such a venture. In fact, many young people get so enthusiastic, they come to prefer saving their money to purchase another share of stock share rather than buy a new pair of designer jeans.

Some families set their teens to studying about stock trading, and then organize a simulated contest to see who makes the best investments over time. Kids love this kind of competition.

Think about how you are preparing your own children to be the investors of tomorrow.

Have a Vision to Take Your Company to the Stock Exchange

Could your company go public and be part of the stock exchange? At this time, as you are first starting out, it may seem like a farfetched dream, but no dream is out of reach if your heart is moved in that direction.

Many entrepreneurs begin small, never imagining that they would one day become a giant corporation. (A great example is the internet billionaire and philanthropist Bill Gates, the founder of Microsoft which he started in his garage. Or Facebook founder Mark Zuckerberg, who began his wildly successful site from a college dorm room. And there are many more, from Amazon to WhatsApp—they all began small and grew to be giants.)

No dream is out of reach if you have a good product, and grow your business with wisdom and insight. Attaining the size and credibility that permit you to do an offering and see your own company represented on the stock exchange certainly takes time, mentoring, strategy, and of course lots of success. But every company starts somewhere.

Many companies can and will grow into public-traded entities, or at least grow to a size that they can be sold for a great profit. You cannot know your outcome at the outset. But you can found your company well, manage it with passion, and see where it goes.

~PART III~
FINANCIAL MASTERY

Keep More of Your Money and Make It Work Hard For You

Financial Mastery

In Part II, you were introduced to many ideas for creating multiple streams of income. This, as has been stated, is crucial for you to attain the level of wealth that will give you the type of lifestyle that is best for you. However, it's not enough to know how to build wealth; it's not even enough to know how to create several businesses and have them all working for you. It's one thing to make money; it's an entirely different matter to *keep what you have earned.*

This section will help you to understand this concept. How sad it is to see hard-working people lose all that they have simply because they didn't know to take these essential steps to protect their wealth.

We live in a litigious society where frivolous lawsuits are almost a way of life. There's a saying that, if you have never been sued, it's because the world perceives that you don't have very much money. Once your wealth begins to build, you become a more compelling target for sue-happy people. It's important that you learn how to put up an impenetrable wall that can protect you and your holdings.

A lot of people are *rich yesterday and poor today* because they knew how to make money, but never learned how to protect it and keep it. Don't let that happen to you.

You can set systems in place, and use the structures of setting up corporations in order to separate you from lawsuits. It is also important that you choose the right insurance coverage to keep your assets safe. If you have worked hard for your money (and I'm sure you have), you will have to agree that it makes sense for you to work hard to protect it to the best of your ability.

Chapter 14

Asset & Personal Protection

Better to be Safe than Sorry

The time to think about and plan for protecting yourself and your assets is <u>way before</u> you ever need it. Always be thinking about how you can be prepared. As the old saying goes: *Plan for the Best, But Prepare for the worst.* Thinking such thoughts as "That will never happen to me" is foolish and unwise. Hopefully, disaster will never strike your home, your business, or your personal wellbeing. That would be wonderful, and life can be so great. But bad things <u>can</u> happen to good people; they happen every day, in fact. It is always better to be safe than sorry.

One important step to take is to create your business (or businesses) with the structures of either a corporation, a partnership, or an LLC (Limited Liability Company). Each one of these, by definition, remains separate from your personal accounts and property. Every company that you found is separate and apart from you. A big mistake often made by start-up entrepreneurs is to jump in and start a business in their own personal name and then begin to use their personal credit. This can backfire on you. Better to take a bit more time, use more caution, and set up your company with formality.

There are other, easier alternatives to setting yourself up as a corporation or LLC. However, if you choose to structure your business as a sole proprietorship or partnership, your personal credit information could be included on your business credit report—and vice-versa. Also realize that, when you are the sole proprietor or partner in a partnership, you will be personally liable for the debts of the business. This means that all of your personal assets are at risk in the event of litigation. The first wall of defense protection for your business is to keep it as an entity that is separate from your personal assets.

Creating Business Credit

There are only two types of credit—personal credit and business (or corporate) credit. Most people are familiar only with personal credit. It's a common practice to use your social security number and apply for a loan or a lease, or to apply for a personal credit card(s).

It's a frightening thing that 92% of small-business owners start out using their personal credit as a way to grow their business. Because of this unwise practice they stand to possibly damage their credit every time they:

- ➢ Apply for business credit with their social security number
- ➢ Run up balances on personal credit cards or credit lines
- ➢ Make cash advances
- ➢ Get declined for credit

Using personal credit to apply for business loans, leases, or credit lines can cause problems in two different ways.

1. It can damage your personal credit score which will then make it more difficult for you to get loans, leases, and credit lines.
2. It can prevent you from building a positive business credit profile – and a good, credible business credit profile is the basis upon which you will build and grow your business in the long run.

A typical entrepreneur will wind up with more than ten credit inquiries a year. This means that you are using your personal credit information linked to your social security number every time you apply for credit for your business and you use; hence, every inquiry is recorded on your personal credit report. The result is that your personal credit score goes down.

Add to that the fact that every time you're declined, and every time you accumulate debt, your score goes down yet again. As a consequence, your chances of being approved for home loans, car loans, equity lines, and credit cards decrease. If you are approved, there's a chance that you could be considered a subprime borrower, someone who will be subject to above-market interest rates. This is not a pretty picture.

It's amazing that most business owners are not aware that they can—and should—separate their personal credit from their business credit. I encourage you to do so right from the start.

Using a Living Trust

Creating a living trust in order to protect your personal assets is one of the simplest and easiest methods of asset protection. However, most people think of it as something only for the very wealthy. A living trust is applicable for nearly any level of wealth.

It's called a living trust because it is created while you are alive, and while you are able to make all of the decisions regarding the trust. You can think of the trust like a *wealth container*. You can put most anything into the trust, where it will be protected, but you still retain total control.

For example, you can deed your house to the living trust, and yet can still mortgage it, make updates and repairs, and even rent it out. But if you were to die, the beneficiaries would then own the house—if the trust so stipulated.

There are three entities involved in setting up a trust. The grantor (if you are setting up the trust, you will be the grantor), the trustee (the person who manages the trust assets and follows the trust agreement—this can also be you). The third party is the beneficiary—this is the person who will benefit from the assets that are within the trust. It is possible that the trust will have several entities in each of the categories.

If stocks or other income-producing assets are held within the trust, the grantor will receive the income derived from these assets.

There are a couple of powerful asset protection aspects to setting up a living trust. The first is the fact that, since you are no longer owner of these assets—the trust is the owner—upon your death all contained therein will be free of probate. This means a great savings in taxes.

The other powerful asset protection is the fact that—depending on the type of trust created—the assets transferred to the trust may no longer be susceptible to the hands of creditors, lien holders, or judgment holders. Think of how strong that wall of protection is, and how much money and grief will be spared when it is correctly put in place.

The revocable trust is one that can be changed at any time so long as the grantor is living and is of a sound mind. This means it is flexible, and can be adjusted as circumstances change. And you, as the grantor, are totally in control.

There can also be a successor trustee, but that trustee will have no power or legal right to change the trust. And upon your death, it immediately becomes an irrevocable trust and will stand as it has been set up.

The successor trustee steps in to manage your assets for you when you die or are incapacitated. This person has the legal right to manage your affairs, and thus eliminates probate court. The successor trustee will immediately have the same powers that you as grantor/trustee had to buy, sell, borrow, or transfer the assets inside the trust. Immediate control means that the estate will be transferred to beneficiaries quickly rather than waiting for probate which can take months, and in some cases even years.

When setting up beneficiaries, typically the estate goes go to the surviving spouse. If no surviving spouse exists, then the assets will pass to anyone else who is named in the trust. This can be whomever you name—children, relatives, friends, or even a charitable organization. Any one of these can be the beneficiary of your trust.

Some people erroneously believe that, as long as a legal will is in place, the deceased person's assets will not go into a probate court. Not true. All that a will does is to direct what is to be done with the assets. Once the owner of the asset has died, probate court is the legal process needed to take their name off the title of an asset and put it in the new owner's name. As mentioned, this can take months to move through the already-clogged legal systems.

Insurance

It's easy to bemoan the fact that we feel we are *insurance poor*. There are many different types of insurance. Oftentimes insurance representatives are more interested in selling what will benefit them than what will benefit their clients.

Obviously, there are some types of insurance that are mandatory such as insurance on your car and your home. Also you need to have health insurance, and property insurance if you have a business location. In addition, don't forget life insurance. This is especially important if you are the income-earner for your family. You must think about their welfare should something happen to you.

So what's the answer? How can all of this confusing information be understood and applied correctly to protect your assets?

Life Insurance: The best way to determine how much life insurance should be taken out on you is to analyze exactly what position your family would be in should you die. Evaluate your situation honestly and carefully. There is no need to over-insure; that is just a waste of money. When calculating, be sure to add in funeral costs, too, because these have become exorbitant in recent years. Many life insurance websites offer insurance estimators which will be a great help in your calculations.

Disability Insurance: Accidents happen. They happen to everyone. No one plans to have an accident, but you can plan to be protected, just in case. If your ability to earn an income is jeopardized, it could be devastating for your family. That is why it's doubly important to have streams of income that produce passive income as pointed out in Part II.

However, even these businesses need attention, and if you are out of commission for a time, you want to have suitable insurance coverage to take care of matters until you are back on your feet.

Health Insurance: Medical expenses continue to rise, as do insurance costs. When you opt to go into business for yourself, company health insurance will be a thing of the past. There are many options that have recently come into the picture. One of these is what's known as a Health Savings Account. It provides a method whereby a family can pay into a savings account for future medical costs. Many different plans are now coming into the picture and it would be worth your time to investigate exactly how they work. As long as the money is always spent on medical needs, the money will never be taxed.

Critical-Illness Policy: If for a time you cannot afford health insurance, at best you would be wise to take out a critical-illness policy as a stopgap measure until you can get a fuller coverage policy. In case of something like a heart attack, you will receive a sizable lump sum to pay not only for medical bills, but also for living expenses.

Umbrella Policy: Because you are now a business owner, you will want to have extended coverage that goes beyond the limits of your existing business liability coverage. An umbrella policy is designed to begin at the point your other policies are maxed out.

Business owners typically look to an umbrella policy to create a wall of protection in case someone successfully sues them. This means that there could be a large jury award or a big financial settlement. Having an umbrella policy in place means that you will be protected against this type of financial ruin.

◆◆◆◆◆

This is by no means an exhaustive list of what is needed in the way of insurance coverage to protect your assets. The main point is that, no matter how much you dread forking over that money for such policies, this area can only be overlooked at the detriment of you, your family and your business.

Don't ignore your asset protection. It is all a part of being a responsible business person.

Chapter 15

Taxation Benefits

No matter where you live, taxes are a way of life. In some countries the taxes that are levied against business owners are more stringent than in others. However, having said that, it is equally true that tax deductions and tax shelters are written into the tax codes, and just need to be understood. These are tax breaks that are legally available, and are often designed specifically as incentives for businesses.

Whatever your region and country's tax laws, the important thing is to learn how to take advantage of every legal tax break that you possibly can. Why allow the government to take any more of your hard-earned money than is rightfully theirs? As was stated at the beginning of this section, it's not enough to gain wealth, it's equally important to keep what you have earned. Not overpaying taxes is a case in point.

As you are growing your wealth and as you are growing your business systems, you will want to formulate a team of professionals to work alongside you. One of those professionals must be a reliable, knowledgeable and trustworthy accountant. Your accountant must be someone who not only understands the tax laws of your country, but is also be aware of your businesses, your goals, and the direction that you want your life to take. Only then can this accountant give you sound counsel. This will not be someone to whom you simply hand over your financials and let him take it from there. This should be someone who has a keen interest in you and your endeavours.

A good accountant will know about existing tax shelters and deductions that you may be totally unaware of. Or investments that will serve as tax-deferred opportunities which can allow you the money to grow without being taxed. He should be able to give you a number of options that will considerably reduce what you have to pay out in taxes.

You want to be able to take every legal means available to you and your business to lower your taxes. This is yet another way in which you are keeping the money you earned.

Chapter 16

Retirement

The Retirement Concept

Retirement is an interesting word and an interesting concept. Historically, the concept of retiring from gainful employment at a certain age is relatively new. At one time in our not-too-distant past, farmers worked the land until a son, son-in-law, or sometimes even a daughter took the reins. The same was true with shop owners and business owners. If a son or daughter didn't take over the business, it may have been a nephew or a trusted apprentice who inherited the enterprise. The ageing owner was then supported by the family until death. Pensions and social security were concepts as yet unheard of.

Life expectancy was shorter in that era; the time between being unable to work (due to aging) and the death of that farmer or shop owner consisted of fewer years than it would today.

And Then It Changed

When did things change? How did this idea of working for a season, then retiring for a season, come into being? It goes back to the industrial revolution when the culture changed from being an agrarian/business-owning society to an employed society. Because the factory worker had no farm or business and no family members to rely upon in old age, the answer was to set up workers' pensions. Pensions were designed to support workers in their old age. And even then, the years that a worker would need that pension was a much shorter time frame than today. Those pension plans are very much a thing of the past. Few workers today can rely on pensions as a part of their retirement strategy.

Retirement in the Present

In today's world the idea of retirement is one of looking forward to the *golden years* when one can sleep late, pursue hobbies and favorite pastimes, enjoy grandchildren, travel, and take long cruises to tropical locales. In other words, retirement is a time when one does what one wants to do. Most people spend a lifetime dreaming of these years. But those dreams are seldom firmly established within workable plans. Usually, they are just that—dreams.

Rather than thinking all your life about a time that you call *retirement,* a time in the vague, far-off future, I believe that it is a better plan to achieve the level of wealth that will enable you to live a *retirement-type of life* today. Why put it off? Through the Wealth Action System, the goal is to develop a lifestyle that enables you to do what you want, when you want to do it, and where you want to do it. And to do it all—**now**. Not decades from now.

The various aspects of creating streams of income presented in Part II are designed with this goal in mind. They center around the concept of building your wealth, and keeping as much of that earned wealth as is possible. You do that by using all of the concepts and strategies presented in this book.

By making your decision to become wealthy now, no longer will you fret and worry about having enough on which to retire and enjoy your golden years. All of your years will be *golden years*. Retirement will not mean that you are depending upon some meager government subsidy plan. In fact, it would be a good thing if the word, and the concept of, *retirement* were removed from your thinking altogether.

Plan instead to live a rich, full, active, satisfying life, every day of your life from this moment on.

Chapter 17

Efficient Record-Keeping

Stay on Top of Financials

One of the ways that a business person can actively keep more of the money that they earn is to stay on top of their financials. Entrepreneurs are often visionaries who have a problem with the little details. However, losing track of where money is coming in from, and where it is going out to, is of utmost importance.

As a business owner, your expertise may very well be in activities considered nonfinancial. All the tedium of bookkeeping and accounting may bore you, and so you may find that you habitually avoid these tasks. Nevertheless, no owner/manager can afford to neglect such an important business foundation as good record-keeping. To do so could result in serious consequences.

Examine Your Progress

Running a successful business will stand or fall on your being aware of accurate financial information. Having a current financial picture is the only way for you to examine the progress of your business. Your record-keeping system will give you the information needed to evaluate many of your more important business decisions.

Are You Making a Profit?

What you will need is a simple, timely system of recording and reporting data. Once the system is in place, you can then control what goes on in your company. You will know if you are making a profit. And if not, you'll know why.

Think about all of the time, work and energy that you have poured into your company. Isn't it worthwhile, to be aware of what's going on financially at all times, both positive and negative? If red flags are going up, you want to know before the fact, not after. You need to know soon enough to take constructive action. The truth is, if you can't effectively handle the present, there may not be any future.

Below is a list of what characterizes a basic record-keeping system.

Characteristics:

> - Simple to use
> - Easy to understand
> - Legible
> - Accurate
> - Easy to follow
> - Reliable
> - Consistent
> - Current
> - Self-balancing
> - Provide data and information for management and outsiders
> - Has internal-control features

Additionally, a good record-keeping system should achieve the following objectives:

Objectives

- The books and records should provide a current operating picture of the business for both insiders and outsiders.
- The data and information in the books should be easily translated into operating or financial statements for use by management, bank managers, professional advisers, or the IRS.
- The books and records should be maintained by employees whose responsibilities are clearly defined, controlled, and divided in such a way as to provide effective internal control and a deterrent to mismanagement of funds, embezzlement, and fraud.
- The double-entry bookkeeping system should provide for checks on clerical accuracy of employees and detect any waste or fraud, in addition to providing

accurate, reliable information for financial statements or data for management.

> Well-organized records not only help you to prepare your tax return, but they also help you to answer questions if your return is selected for examination, or help you to prepare a response if you are billed for additional tax.

In the section on taxes it was said that you will need a trusted accountant. If you are not sure how to put together a good record-keeping system, ask your accountant to help you set it up.

However, a word of warning: just because someone else sets it up for you and you put it into operation, that is still no excuse for you not to learn how to understand the numbers and what they all mean. Ignorance is no excuse. If you want to keep more of your money, if you want to run a well-executed and successful business, you must keep your finger on the pulse of how it is functioning at all times.

Chapter 18

How to Make Your Money Work For You

Working Harder and Longer is Not the Answer

I am constantly amazed at the number of people who see that the only way to get ahead financially is to work harder, work more hours, get a raise in pay, get a better job, and so on. In their mind, it's all about trading hours for dollars. Their understanding of how to put money to work for them is extremely limited. And, in some cases, non-existent.

We touched on this concept briefly in Part II. There are a number of ways that you can put your own money to work, such as through investing in the stock market or in other companies, or in purchasing real estate or paper assets that you know will go up in value.

Buy as many paper assets as possible, then let those assets work for you. This takes advantage of leverage, and is truly one of the only ways that a person is going to achieve great wealth.

No matter how much you earn, no matter how high your earning bracket is, trading hours for dollars will never create wealth. It only happens when you understand how to make your money work for you. This involves your understanding how to make wise investments and the concept of compound interest.

So again, it's not how much money you make, it is how much money you keep and how hard you make that money work for you. That is the key to your success and Action Wealth creation.

About the Author

GEOFFREY SEMAGANDA runs a global business-training and consultancy firm that helps companies around the world to run their enterprises more efficiently, productively and profitably.

A respected entrepreneur, speaker, author and philanthropist, he is the founder and CEO of the Action Wealth Group of companies (Action Wealth Academy, Action Wealth Conference, Action Wealth Systems, Action Wealth Real Estate Development) and also a spokesperson for his own non-profit initiatives focusing on Youth Business Development, Clean Water Program and Give Blood.

He has appeared on numerous TV and radio shows all around the world and has educated more

For free personal and business development training programs visit **www.actionwealthacademy.com**

than 500,000 people through his personal and business development courses and live seminars.

Geoffrey started making a profit at the age of nine to support his family during the war in his home country of Uganda. He moved to Europe in his early teens and established his first business at the age of 16; and by the age of 21 he had established five successful businesses in three countries.today he often shares the stage with some of the best personal and business development speakers in the world.

His other books include *Financial Literacy for Teens & their Parents, It's Time for Your Message: How to Position, Package and Promote Yourself as an Expert, 50 Profitable Businesses to Run from Home* and *Lead in Your Chosen Field as a Super Successful Business Consultant*.

You can contact Geoffrey here:
Web: www.actionwealthsystem.com
Email: info@actionwealthsystem.com
Meet Geoffrey, and receive free personal and business development at www.actionwealthacademy.com

Printed in Great Britain
by Amazon.co.uk, Ltd.,
Marston Gate.